THE PLANETS AND STARS

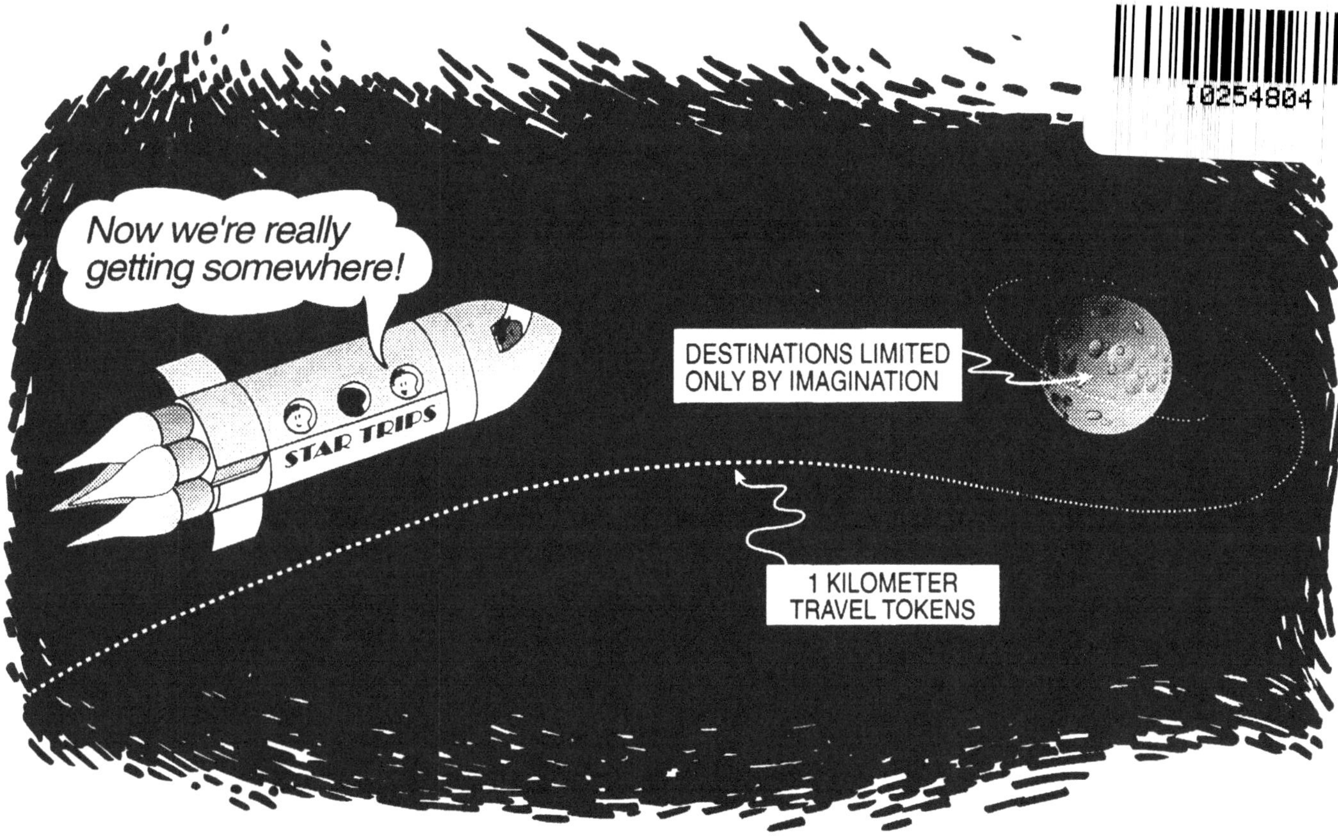

SCIENCE WITH SIMPLE THINGS SERIES

Conceived and written by
RON MARSON

Illustrated by
PEG MARSON

342 S Plumas Street
Willows, CA 95988

www.topscience.org

WHAT CAN YOU COPY?

Dear Educator,

Please honor our copyright restrictions. We offer liberal options and guidelines below with the intention of balancing your needs with ours. When you buy these labs and use them for your own teaching, you sustain our work. If you "loan" or circulate copies to others without compensating TOPS, you squeeze us financially, and make it harder for our small non-profit to survive. Our well-being rests in your hands. Please help us keep our low-cost, creative lessons available to students everywhere. Thank you!

PURCHASE, ROYALTY and LICENSE OPTIONS

TEACHERS, HOMESCHOOLERS, LIBRARIES:

We do all we can to keep our prices low. Like any business, we have ongoing expenses to meet. We trust our users to observe the terms of our copyright restrictions. While we prefer that all users purchase their own TOPS labs, we accept that real-life situations sometimes call for flexibility.

Reselling, trading, or loaning our materials is prohibited unless one or both parties contribute an Honor System Royalty as fair compensation for value received. We suggest the following amounts – let your conscience be your guide.

HONOR SYSTEM ROYALTIES: If making copies from a library, or sharing copies with colleagues, please calculate their value at 50 cents per lesson, or 25 cents for homeschoolers. This contribution may be made at our website or by mail (addresses at the bottom of this page). Any additional tax-deductible contributions to make our ongoing work possible will be accepted gratefully and used well.

Please follow through promptly on your good intentions. Stay legal, and do the right thing.

SCHOOLS, DISTRICTS, and HOMESCHOOL CO-OPS:

PURCHASE Option: Order a book in quantities equal to the number of target classrooms or homes, and receive quantity discounts. If you order 5 books or downloads, for example, then you have unrestricted use of this curriculum for any 5 classrooms or families per year for the life of your institution or co-op.

- **2-9 copies of any title:** 90% of current catalog price + shipping.
- **10+ copies of any title:** 80% of current catalog price + shipping.

ROYALTY/LICENSE Option: Purchase just one book or download *plus* photocopy or printing rights for a designated number of classrooms or families. If you pay for 5 additional Licenses, for example, then you have purchased reproduction rights for an entire book or download edition for any **6** classrooms or families per year for the life of your institution or co-op.

- **1-9 Licenses:** 70% of current catalog price per designated classroom or home.
- **10+ Licenses:** 60% of current catalog price per designated classroom or home.

WORKSHOPS and TEACHER TRAINING PROGRAMS:

We are grateful to all of you who spread the word about TOPS. Please limit copies to only those lessons you will be using, and collect all copyrighted materials afterward. No take-home copies, please. Copies of copies are strictly prohibited.

Copyright © 1995 by TOPS Learning Systems. All rights reserved. This material is created/printed/transmitted in the United States of America. No part of this program may be used, reproduced, or transmitted in any manner whatsoever without written permission from the publisher, *except as explicitly stated above and below*:

The ***original owner*** of this book or digital download is permitted to make multiple copies of all ***student materials*** for per-sonal teaching use, provided all reproductions bear copyright notice. A purchasing school or homeschool co-op may assign ***one*** purchased book or digital download to ***one*** teacher, classroom, family, or study group ***per year***. Reproduction of student materials from libraries is permitted if the user compensates TOPS as outlined above. Reproduction of any copyrighted ma-terials for commercial sale is prohibited.

For licensing, honor system royalty payments, contact: **www.TOPScience.org**; or **TOPS Learning Systems 342 S Plumas St, Willows CA 95988**; or inquire at **customerservice@topscience.org**

ISBN 978-0-941008-41-9

CONTENTS

 **PART I — PREPARATION AND SUPPORT**

A. A TOPS Teaching Model
C. Getting Ready
D. Gathering Materials
E. Sequencing Activities
F. Long Range Objectives
G. Review / Test Questions

 **PART II — ACTIVITIES AND LESSON NOTES**

1. Landmarks
2. Pointer Box
3. Sun Declinations
4. Follow that Star
5. Earth in a Jar
6. Ocean in a Jar
7. Dipper Box
8. Polar Graph
9. Apparent Size
10. Lots-o-Dots
11. Light Lightning
12. Star Travel
13. Our Solar System
14. Sky Sphere
15. The Zodiac
16. Star Search
17. Proportional Planets
18. Elbow Room
19. The Wanderers
20. Our Milky Way

 **PART III — SUPPLEMENTARY CUTOUTS**

1 / landmark maps
2 / earth circle • 4 / shadow screen • 6 / round map • 8 / sun arrow
2 / concept list • 5 / concept list
3 / sun protractor
5 / long maps • 5 / short map • 5 / compass circle
6 / concept table • 14 / concept list
7 / big dipper
7 / view point
8 / polar graph
9 / angle finder • 12 / star ruler
10 / lots-o-dots
11 / kilometer bar
13 / solar system squares • 13 / sun ruler
14 / north stars
14 / south stars
15 / zodiac ring
15 / sky tabs • 17 / earth ruler • 19 / planet finder
16 / concept list • 19 / concept list
16 / star dictionary
16 / sky wheel
20 / milky way disk • 20 / galaxy ruler

A TOPS Teaching Model

If science were only a set of explanations and a collection of facts, you could teach it with blackboard and chalk. You could require students to read chapters in a textbook, assign questions at the end of each chapter, and set periodic written exams to determine what they remember. Science is traditionally taught in this manner. Everybody studies the same information at the same time. Class togetherness is preserved.

But science is more than this. It is also process — a dynamic interaction of rational inquiry and creative play. Scientists probe, poke, handle, observe, question, think up theories, test ideas, jump to conclusions, make mistakes, revise, synthesize, communicate, disagree and discover. Students can understand science as process only if they are free to think and act like scientists, in a classroom that recognizes and honors individual differences.

Science is *both* a traditional body of knowledge *and* an individualized process of creative inquiry. Science as process cannot ignore tradition. We stand on the shoulders of those who have gone before. If each generation reinvents the wheel, there is no time to discover the stars. Nor can traditional science continue to evolve and redefine itself without process. Science without this cutting edge of discovery is a static, dead thing.

Here is a teaching model that combines both the content and process of science into an integrated whole. This model, like any scientific theory, must give way over time to new and better ideas. We challenge you to incorporate this TOPS model into your own teaching practice. Change it and make it better so it works for *you*.

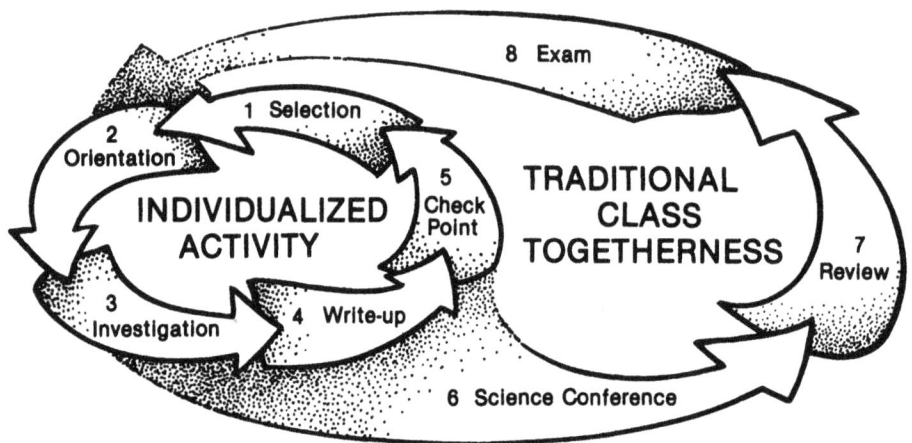

1. SELECTION

Students generally select worksheets in sequence, because new concepts build on old ones in a specific order. There are, however, exceptions to this pattern: students might *skip* a lesson that is not challenging; *repeat* a lesson with doubtful results; *add* an experiment to answer their own "what-would-happen-if?" questions.

Working at their own pace, students fall into a natural routine that creates stability and order. They still have questions and problems, to be sure, but remain purposefully engaged with a definite sense of direction.

2. ORIENTATION

Any student with basic reading skills can successfully interpret our carefully designed worksheet directions. If your class is new to TOPS, it may take a while for your students to get used to following directions by themselves, and to trust in their own problem-solving ability.

When students ask you for help, first ask them to read what they don't understand. If they didn't read the instruction in the first place, this should clear things up. Identify poor readers in your class. When they ask, "What does this mean?" they may be asking in reality, "Will you please read these directions aloud?"

Beyond reading comprehension, certain basic concepts and skills are also necessary to complete many worksheets. You can't, for example, ask students to measure something unless they know how to use a ruler. *Supporting Concepts* in our Teaching Notes list these basics plus strategies for teaching them. Teach these prerequisites at the beginning of class periods, before students begin their daily individualized work. Anticipate the needs and abilities of your particular age group: primary students will need more introductory support than middle school students; secondary students may require none at all.

3. INVESTIGATION

Students work through the worksheets independently and cooperatively. They follow their own experimental strategies and help each other. You can encourage this behavior by helping students only *after* they have tried to help themselves. As a resource teacher, you work to stay *out* of the center of attention, responding to student questions rather than posing teacher questions.

Some students will progress more rapidly through these worksheets than others. To finish as a cohesive group, announce well in advance when individualized worksheet activity will end. Expect to generate a frenzy of activity as students rush to meet your deadline. While slower students finish the core activities you specify, challenge your more advanced students with open-ended *Extension* activities from our teaching notes, or to design their own original experiments.

4. WRITE-UP

Underlined numbers in the worksheets signal that students should explain the how and why of things with answers written on their own papers. Answers may be brief and to the point, with the exception of those that require creative writing. Students may accelerate their pace by completing these reports out of class.

Students may work alone, or in cooperative lab groups. But each one should prepare an original write-up, and bring it to you for approval. Avoid an avalanche of write-ups near the end of the module by enforcing this simple rule: each write-up must be approved *before* starting the next activity.

5. CHECK POINT

Student and teacher together evaluate each write-up on a pass/no-pass basis. Thus no time is wasted haggling over grades. If the student has made reasonable effort consistent with individual ability, check off the completed activity on a progress chart. Students keep these in notebooks or assignment folders kept on file in class.

Because the student is present when you evaluate, feedback is immediate and effective. A few moments of your personal attention is surely more effective than tedious margin notes that students may not heed or understand. Remember, you don't have to point out every error. Zero in on particular weaknesses. If reasonable effort is not evident, direct students to make specific improvements and return for a final check.

A responsible lab assistant can double the amount of individual attention each student receives. If he or she is mature and respected by your students, have the assistant check even-numbered reports, while you check the odd ones. This will balance the work load and assure that everyone receives equal treatment.

6. SCIENCE CONFERENCE

Individualized worksheet activity has ended. This is a time for students to come together, to discuss experimental results, to debate and draw conclusions. Slower students learn about the enrichment activities of faster classmates. Those who did original investigations or made unusual discoveries share this information with their peers, just like scientists at a real conference.

This conference is an opportunity to expand ideas, explore relevancy, and integrate subject areas. Consider bringing in films, newspaper articles and community speakers. It's a meaningful time to investigate the technological and social implications of the topic you are studying. Make it an event!

7. REVIEW

Does your school have an adopted science textbook? Do parts of your science syllabus still need to be covered? Now is the time to integrate traditional science resources into your overall program. Your students already share a common background of hands-on lab work. With this base of experience, they can now read the text with greater understanding, think and problem-solve more successfully, communicate more effectively.

You might spend just a day here, or an entire week. Finish with a review of major concepts in preparation for the final exam. Our review/test questions provide an excellent basis for discussion and study.

8. EXAM

Use any combination of our review/test questions, plus questions of your own, to determine how well students have mastered the concepts they've been learning. Those who finish your exam early might be eager to begin work in the next new TOPS module.

Now that your class has completed a major TOPS learning cycle, it's time to start fresh with a brand new topic. Those who messed up and got behind don't need to stay there. Everyone begins the new topic on an equal footing. This frequent change of pace encourages your students to work hard, to enjoy what they learn, and thereby grow in scientific literacy.

Getting Ready

Here is a checklist of things to think about and preparations to make before beginning your first lesson on THE PLANETS AND STARS.

✔ Review the scope and sequence.

Take just a few minutes, right now, to page through all 20 lessons. Pause to read each *Objective* (top left corner of the Teaching Notes) and scan each lesson.

✔ Set aside appropriate class time.

Allow an average of perhaps 1 class period per lesson (more for younger students), plus time at the end of this module for discussion, review and testing. If you teach science every day, this module will likely engage your class for about 5 weeks. If your schedule doesn't allow this much science, consult the logic tree on page E to see which activities you can safely omit without breaking conceptual links between lessons.

✔ Decide when to start.

Teach this astronomy module during any season of the year, at any time of day. If you teach science every day, an optimal time to begin is a day or two before a first quarter moon. By the time your students make their first night sky observations in activity 9, the moon will rise late enough to insure dark evening skies. As students begin more extensive sky observations in activity 16, the moon will be new, providing the darkest possible sky for clear viewing. Don't despair if city lights, smog, clouds or fog obscure the stars. Nearly every lesson works fine without stars. And you have the perfect excuse to take an evening field trip into the countryside.

✔ Number your activity sheet masters.

The small number printed in the top right corner of each activity sheet shows its position within the series. If this ordering fits your schedule, copy each number into the blank parentheses next to it. Be sure to use pencil; you may decide to revise, rearrange, add or omit lessons the next time you teach this module. Insert your own better ideas wherever they fit best, and renumber the sequence. This allows your curriculum to adapt and grow as you do.

✔ Photocopy sets of student activity sheets.

All activity sheets in this module can be reused. Photocopy and collate a classroom set to use year after year, as you would any textbook. All questions emphasized with <u>underlined numbers</u> require students to respond on separate paper. Find all supplementary materials that support each lesson on reproducible pages at the back of this module. The *Materials* list that accompanies each lesson tells you when these cutouts are needed, and how many to photocopy.

Please observe our copyright notice at the front of this module. We allow you, the purchaser, to make as many copies as you need, but forbid supplying your materials to other teachers for use in other classrooms. Our only income is from the sale of these inexpensive modules. If you would like to help spread the word that TOPS is tops, please request multiple copies of our TOPS Ideas magazine/catalog (sent to you free and postpaid) to distribute to other faculty members or student teachers. These offer a variety of sample lessons and an order form, so your colleagues can purchase their own TOPS modules.

✔ Collect needed materials.

See page D for details.

✔ Organize a way to track assignments.

Keep student work on file in class. If you lack a file cabinet, a box with a brick will serve. File folders or notebooks both make suitable assignment organizers. Students will feel a sense of accomplishment as they see their folders grow heavy, or their notebooks fill, with completed assignments. Since all papers stay together, reference and review are easy.

Ask students to number a sheet of paper from 1 to 20 and tape it inside the front cover of their folders or notebooks. Track individual progress through this module (and future modules) by initialing lesson numbers as completed.

✔ Review safety procedures.

In our litigation-conscious society, we find that publishers are often more committed to protecting themselves from liability suits than protecting students from physical hazards. Lab instructions are so often filled with spurious advisories, cautions and warnings that students become desensitized to safety in general. If we cry "Wolf!" too often, real warnings of present danger may go unheeded.

At TOPS we endeavor to use good sense in deciding what students already know (don't stab yourself in the eye) and what they should be told (don't look directly at the sun.) Scissors and pins, of course, could be dangerous in the hands of unsupervised children. This curriculum cannot anticipate irresponsible behavior or negligence. It is ultimately the teacher's responsibility to see that common-sense safety rules are followed at all times. And it is your students' responsibility to respect and protect themselves and each other.

Unusual hazards detailed in this module are as follows:
• In activity 1, consider safety as a criterion for selecting a home star-watching site. Activity 9, step 7, encourages family involvement in this activity.
• Never sight directly into the sun. Use shadows to aim the Pointer Straw at the sun as detailed in activity 4.
• If you're working with young children, provide blunt scissors for the dot-cutting in activity 10. Supervise!

✔ Communicate your grading expectations.

Whatever your grading philosophy, your students need to understand how they will be assessed. Here is a scheme that counts individual effort, attitude and overall achievement. We think these three components deserve equal weight:
• Pace (effort): Tally the number of check points and extra credit experiments you have initialed for each student. Low-ability students should be able to keep pace with gifted students, since write-ups are evaluated relative to individual performance standards on a pass/no-pass basis. Students with absences or those who tend to work slowly might assign themselves more homework out of class.
• Participation (attitude): This is a subjective grade, assigned to measure personal initiative and responsibility. Active participators who work to capacity receive high marks. Inactive onlookers who waste time in class and copy the results of others receive low marks.
• Exam (achievement): Activities point toward generalizations that provide a basis for hypothesizing and predicting. The test questions on pages G-J will help you assess whether students understand relevant theory and can apply it in a predictive way.

Gathering Materials

Listed below is everything you'll need to teach this module. You probably already have most items. Buy the rest locally, or ask students to bring recycled materials from home.

Keep this classification key in mind as you review what's needed.

general on-the-shelf materials:	*special in-a-box materials:*
Normal type suggests that these materials are used often. Keep these basics on shelves or in drawers that are readily accessible to your students. The next TOPS module you teach will likely utilize many of these same materials.	Italic type suggests that these materials are unusual. Keep these specialty items in a separate box. After you finish teaching this module, label the box for storage and put it away, ready to use again.
(substituted materials):	*optional materials:
Parentheses enclosing any item suggests a ready substitute. These alternatives may work just as well as the original. Don't be afraid to improvise, to make do with what you have.	An asterisk sets these items apart. They are nice to have, but you can easily live without them. They are probably not worth an extra trip to the store, unless you are gathering other materials as well.

Everything is listed in order of first use. Start gathering at the top of this list and work down. Ask students to bring recycled items from home. The Teaching Notes may occasionally suggest additional *Extensions*. Materials for these optional experiments are listed neither here nor under *Materials*. Read the extension itself to determine what new items, if any, are required.

Quantities depend on how many students you have, how you organize them into activity groups, and how you teach. Decide which of these 3 estimates best applies to you, then adjust quantities up or down as necessary:

$Q_1/Q_2/Q_3$
- **Single Student:** Enough for 1 student to do all the experiments.
- **Individualized Approach:** Enough for 30 students informally working in pairs, all self-paced.
- **Traditional Approach:** Enough for 30 students, organized into pairs, all doing the same lesson.

KEY:	*special in-a-box materials* (substituted materials)	general on-the-shelf materials *optional materials

$Q_1/Q_2/Q_3$

1/15/15	scissors — younger children should use blunt scissors in activity 10	.1/1/1	cup oil-based modeling clay
1/8/8	rolls masking tape	1/1/1	bottle food coloring with dropper dispenser — blue is best color
1/2/8	meter sticks	1/1/1	roll plastic wrap
1/1/1	wall clock (wristwatches)	1/30/30	flashlights filtered with *red cellophane, red plastic from shopping bag, or red tissue paper* — students will use these at home
1/1/1	pkg. standard 1 inch straight pins		
1/1/1	*pkg. extra long pins — about 1.5 inches		
2/30/30	Post Grape Nuts cereal boxes, 32 oz. size or equivalent — see notes 2	1/5/15	hand lenses
		1/1/1	stack of standard-sized newspaper 3 feet high — see note 11
1/5/15	pennies		
1/5/5	rolls clear tape	1/5/15	each, yellow and black crayons or markers
2/30/30	straight plastic straws, 1/4 inch in diameter or slightly smaller	3/63/75	paper plates, standard 9 inch diameter with traditional rippled border
1/1/1	box standard-sized paper clips	1/5/15	drawing compasses
1/3/8	paper punch tools	1/1/1	*shaker of black pepper*
1/1/1	spool of thread	1/1/1	*container of coarse sand with pebbles*
1/5/15	metal washers, any size	1/5/15	tennis balls, new or used
1/5/15	*lbs. gravel, large rocks or bricks	1/1/1	roll heavy string
1/15/15	baby food jars with tight-fitting lids — use 4 oz. size only, with basic cylindrical shape	1/2/2	*pkg. clothespins
		1/1/1	copy of The World Almanac and Book of Facts, or equivalent reference
1/5/15	*graduated cylinder, 50 ml		
1/1/1	*roll paper towels	1/1/1	*a current calendar with moon phases
1/3/8	*bottles white glue	1/1/1	ball of cotton

Sequencing Activities

This logic tree shows how all the activities in this module tie together. In general, students begin at the trunk of the tree and work up through the related branches. Lower level activities support the ones above.

You may, at your discretion, omit certain activities or change their sequence to meet specific class needs. However, when leaves open *vertically* into each other, those below logically precede those above, and cannot be omitted.

When possible, students should complete the activities in the same sequence as numbered. If time is short, however, or certain students need to catch up, you can use this logic tree to identify concept-related *horizontal* activities. Some of these might be omitted since they serve to reinforce learned concepts rather than introduce new ones.

For whatever reason, when you wish to make sequence changes, you'll find this logic tree a valuable reference. Parentheses in the upper right corner of each worksheet allow you total flexibility. They are blank so you can pencil in sequence numbers of your own choosing.

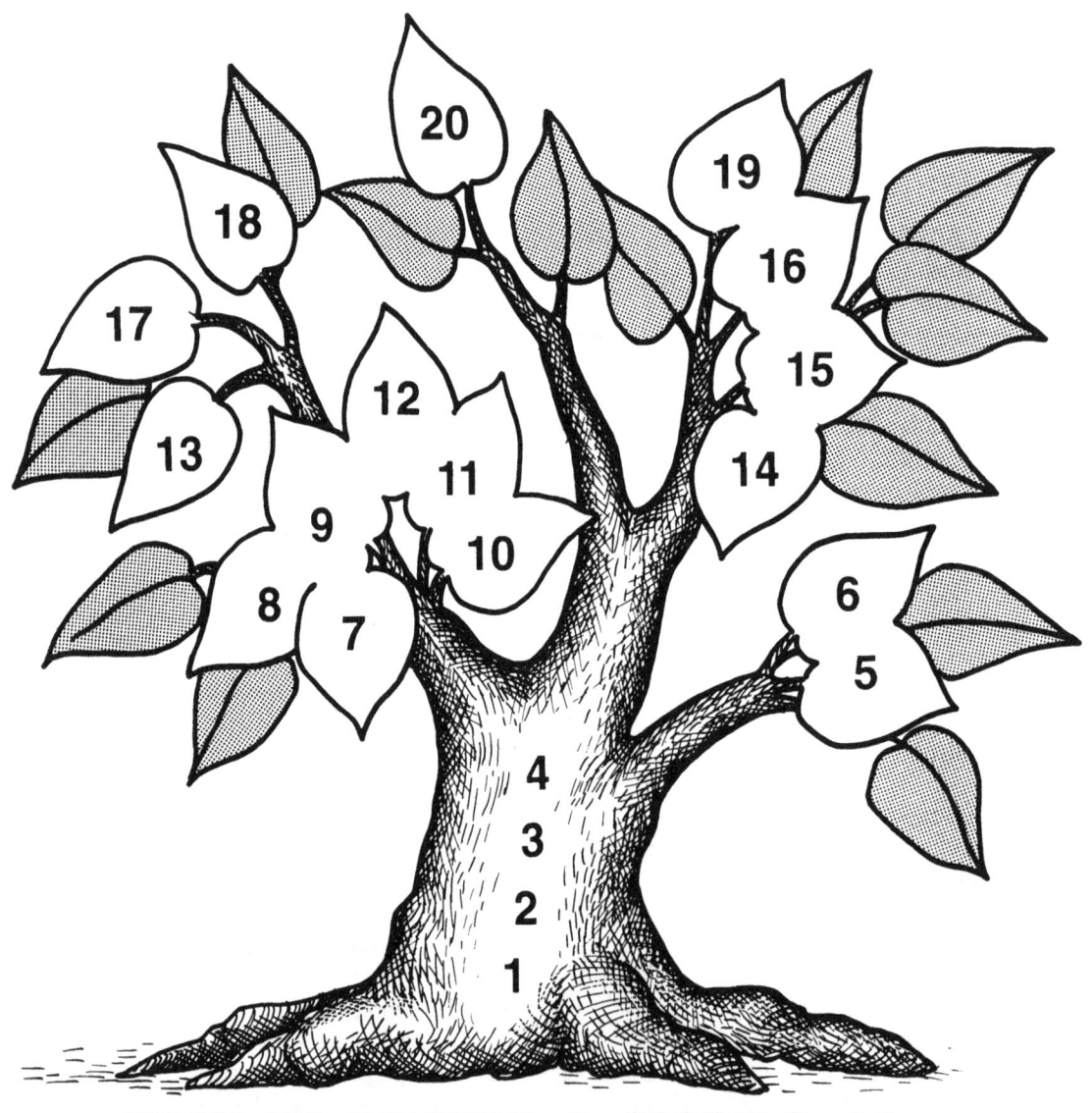

THE PLANETS & STARS 41

Long-Range Objectives

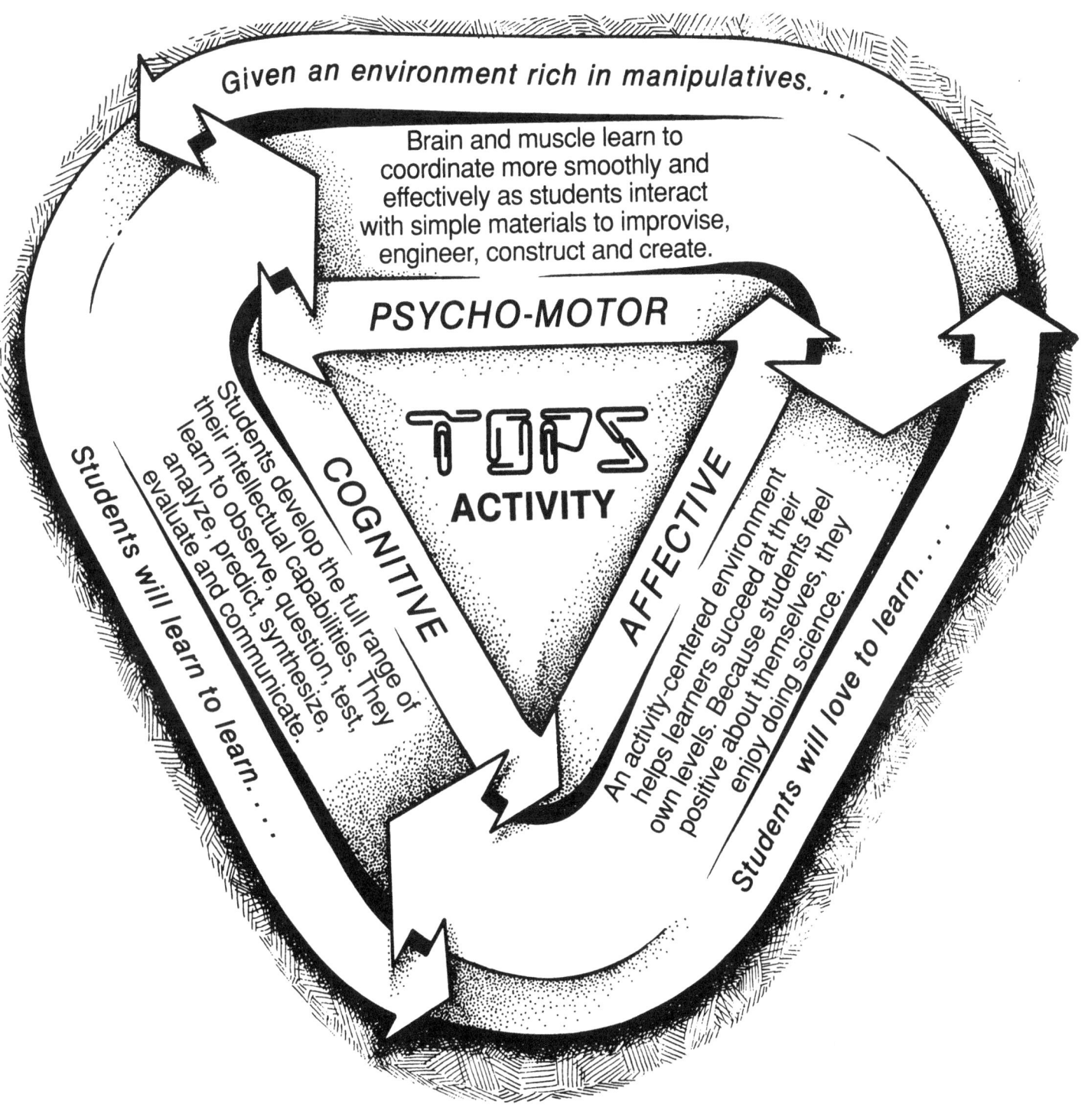

Review / Test Questions

Photocopy both pages of test questions. Cut out those questions you wish to use and tape them onto clean paper. Include questions of your own design, as well. Crowd them all onto a single page for students to answer on another paper, or leave space for student responses after each question, as you wish. Duplicate a class set and your custom-made test is ready to use. Use leftover questions as a class review in preparation for the final exam.

activity 1-2
Write the direction on each point of this compass rose:

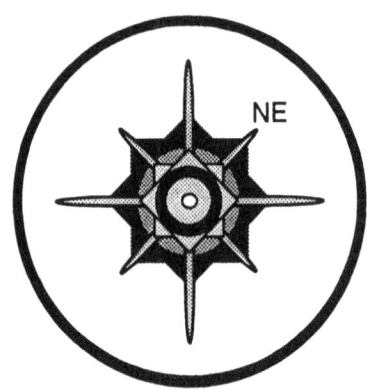

activity 1-3
Dwayne lives on the North American plains. He sees the sun rise in the northeast at 5:40 am and set in the northwest at 7:50 pm.
a. Compute Dwayne's high noon to the nearest minute.
b. Where does Dwayne's shadow point at this time? Where is the sun in the sky?
c. Is there snow on the ground? Explain your answer.

activity 1-4
Required: Pointer Box with Sun Protractor.
a. Trace the path of the sun at your latitude from sunrise to sunset for a calendar date of September 1. Briefly describe what you did.
b. What is the sun's declination on September 1? Where does it rise and set?

activity 1,5,6
You are lost in the high Oregon desert without a compass.
a. How would you locate N, S, E and W during the day?
b. How would you find your way by night?

activity 2,3,4
Hold your thumb at a right angle to your index finger. Explain how to use this hand to trace your celestial equator.

activity 3
Optional: Sun Protractor.
Name the 4 special days that begin the 4 seasons. What are the declinations of the sun at these times of year?

activity 3-6
Sara is looking at the rings of Saturn in her new telescope. Leaving everything in place, she goes to find her brother Raul so he can look, too. After a while they both return. Raul looks into the telescope without disturbing its alignment, but sees no Saturn! What happened?

activity 4-5
The sun and stars appear to arc across your sky from east to west once a day. What is really happening?

activity 5-6 A
A camera, set up in Ohio, is aimed at different parts of the starry sky. Its shutter is left open so the circling stars leave trails on the exposed film. At what part of the sky did the camera point to take each of these pictures?

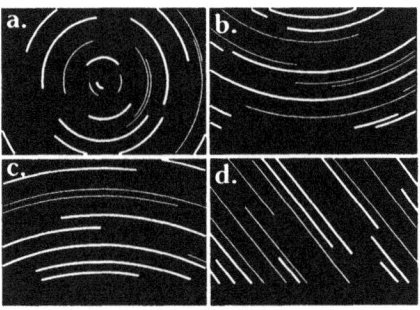

activity 5-6 B
Required: Star Jar.
Name the month of the year when...
a. the sun is "in" Orion.
b. Orion culminates at sunset.
c. Orion culminates at midnight.
d. Orion culminates at sunrise.

activity 7,9
Make your little finger *appear* larger than your thumb. How did you did this?

activity 7,12
Required: Dipper Box with Star Ruler.
Locate these pairs of star on your Dipper box: Megrez-Phecda, Phecda-Dubhe.
a. Measure the apparent separation between each star pair.
b. Measure the actual separation between each star pair.
c. Are star distances as they appear in the night sky? Explain.

activity 7,9,14
Does your Sky Sphere model the *actual* position of the stars in space, or their *apparent* positions in the sky? What about your Dipper Box?

activity 8 A
Required: Polar Graph.
What are the coordinates of Alkaid at the end of the Dipper's handle? State the name of each coordinate as well as its value.

activity 8 B
Required: Polar Graph.
a. Plot the position of the star Alderamin (in the constellation Cepheus) on your Polar Graph. It has a sidereal time of 21.3 hours and a declination of 63° N.
b. What constellation could you use as a "signpost" to find Alderamin? Explain.

activity 8,9
Optional: Polar Graph
You can model the motion of the Big Dipper and Cassiopeia in our night sky with an umbrella. Explain how to do this.

activity 9
The fingers of your outstretched hand match the angle of separation between certain stars in the Big Dipper. Label both drawings to show this correspondence.

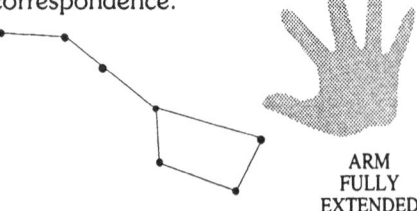
ARM FULLY EXTENDED

activity 10
How many dots are in this grid?

activity 10-11
A million dots are printed in a perfect square. How many rows and columns are there?

activity 11

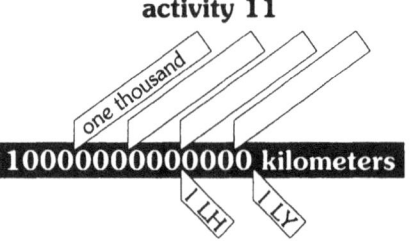

a. Fill in the 3 empty boxes on this Kilometer Bar.
b. The distances that light travels in 1 hour and in 1 year are marked at the bottom. According to this bar, how many times farther does light travel in 1 year than in 1 hour?

Answers

activity 1-2

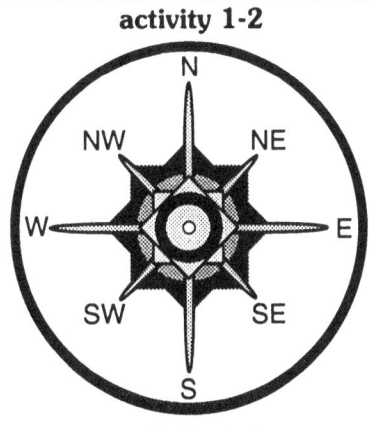

activity 1-3

a.
SUNRISE	SUNSET
5:40 am	7:50pm
(+ 20 min)	(-20 min)
6:00 am	7:30 pm
(+ 7 hrs)	(-7 hrs)
1:00 pm	12:30 pm
(- 15 min)	(+15 min)
12:45 pm	12:45 pm

↖ high noon ↗

b. Dwayne's shadow points due North at high noon. The sun has culminated above Dwayne's southern horizon.
c. Snow is not likely in the spring or summer: there are now over 14 hours of daylight; the sun is rising in the NE and setting in the NW.

activity 1-4

a. Adjust the angle between straws to match the declination corresponding to the beginning of September on the Sun Protractor. Align your Pointer Box to its N landmark so the Polaris Straw points to Polaris. Sweep the Sun Straw from east to west to trace the path of the sun.
b. The sun's declination on the first of September is 9° N. The sun rises north of due east and sets north of due west on that day.

activity 1,5,6

a. At high noon, halfway between sunrise and sunset, face the direction that your shadow points. You now face north; south is at your back; east on your right; west on your left.
b. Find Polaris in the night sky. This star is always fixed in the sky above your N horizon. Find all other directions from this reference point.

activity 2,3,4

Point your index finger to Polaris while rotating your hand right and left. Your thumb (still at a right angle) traces out your celestial equator from horizon to horizon.

activity 3

spring equinox: sun deci. = 0°.
summer solstice: sun deci. = 23.5° N.
fall equinox: sun deci. = 0°.
winter solstice: sun deci. = 23.5° S.

activity 3-6

The telescope no longer points at Saturn. While Sara was looking for Raul, the rotating earth moved the telescope out of alignment.

activity 4-5

The earth is really rotating on its axis once a day, sweeping you under the stars in the opposite direction, from west to east.

activity 5-6 A

The camera was aimed...
a. at the NCP.
b. at the northern horizon.
c. at the southern horizon.
d. at the western horizon.

activity 5-6 B

a. June
b. March
c. December
d. September.

activity 7,9

Hold your little finger near one eye with the other eye closed. Hold your thumb farther away. The little finger now appears larger than the thumb because it is closer to your eye.

activity 7,12

a. Measuring with the Degrees side of the Star Ruler gives these APPARENT separations:
   Megrez-Phecda = 4.2°
   Phecda-Dubhe = 9.5°
b. Measuring with the Light Years side of the Star Ruler gives these ACTUAL separations:
   Megrez-Phecda = 26 LY
   Phecda-Dubhe = 20 LY
c. No. Widely separated stars might appear close together only because they are together in your line of sight. Megrez and Phecda, for example, are not actually closer, just apparently closer.

activity 7,9,14

The Sky Sphere models the *apparent* positions of the stars in the sky. The cup and handle on the Dipper Box also models the *apparent* positions of these stars. In addition, the pin heads model the *actual* positions of these stars in space.

activity 8 A

sidereal time = 13.8 h
declination = 49° N

activity 8 B

a.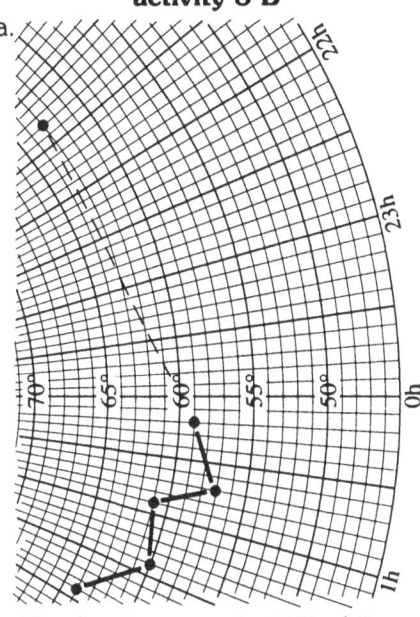

b. The first 2 stars in the "M" of Cassiopeia (or the last 2 stars in the "W") point the way to Alderamin.

activity 8,9

Optional: Polar Graph.
Draw the Big Dipper and Cassiopeia on separate pieces of paper. Pin them to an open umbrella in the same relative positions they have on your Polar Graph, with Polaris in the middle. Point the umbrella at Polaris and turn it east to west (counterclockwise).

activity 9

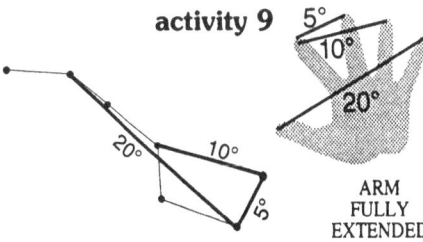

activity 10

9 rows x 13 columns = 117 dots

activity 10-11

There are 1,000 rows and columns:
1,000 rows x 1,000 columns = 1,000,000 dots.

activity 11

a.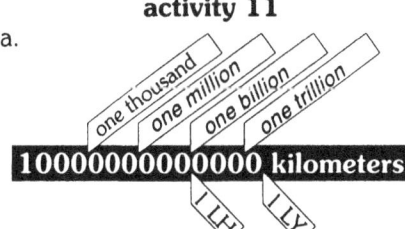

b. Four zeros separate 1 LH from 1 LY. Light travels about 10,000 times farther.

Review / Test Questions (continued)

activity 10-12 A
a. A full sheet of newspaper printed with Lots-o-Dots contains exactly 1 million dots. Write out this number with the correct number of zeros.
b. Light travels about 10 trillion kilometers in 1 year. Write out this number with the correct number of zeros.
c. If each dot is a token good for 1 kilometer, how many sheets of dots do you need to travel 1 Light Year?

activity 10-12 B
Light takes 500 seconds to travel from the sun to the earth.
a. A solar flare happens on the sun. How many *minutes* pass before we can detect this event on earth?
b. Light travels 300,000 k/second. How far away is the sun in kilometers?
c. How would you represent this distance with Lots-o-Dots?

activity 12
In our part of the Milky Way, stars are scattered through space with an average separation of about 7 LY.
a. Traveling at the speed of light, how long would it take, on average, to travel from star to star?
b. How many earth years would it take to visit every star in an average cube of space that measures 70 LY on a side?

activity 13
Required: Solar Squares.

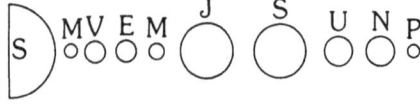

Earth's orbit is drawn around a crossmark representing the sun's position. Sketch in the orbits of Venus, Mars and Jupiter at the correct scale. Label them V, M and J.

activity 13,18
Required: Solar Squares.
What is useful about this model of our solar system? What is misleading?

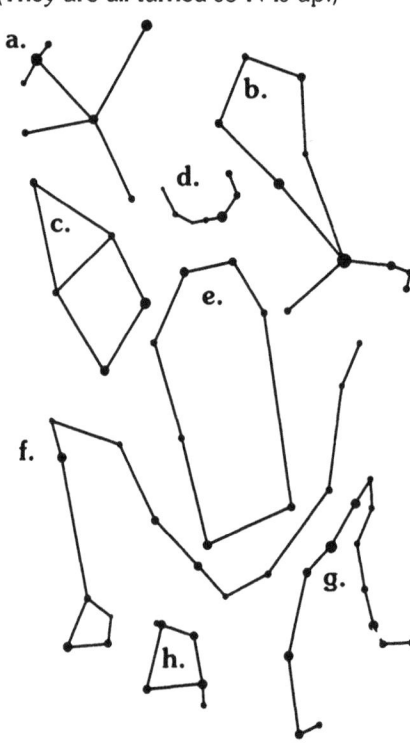

activity 14-16
Optional: Sky Sphere or Star Jar
Describe how each constellation appears to move at your home latitude.
a. Cassiopeia.
b. Orion.
c. The Southern Cross.

activity 15-16 A
Optional: Sky Sphere
a. Draw any 4 of these 8 constellations: Sagittarius, Capricornus, Taurus, Gemini, Auriga, Canis Major, Ursa Minor, Cygnus.
b. Which of these constellations are part of the zodiac?

activity 15-16 B
Required: Sky Sphere
Identify these constellations by name. (They are all turned so N is up.)

activity 16
Describe the path of your meridian from the NCP to your horizon.

activity 17
Required: Solar Squares and a penny.
If the earth is as big as a penny...
a. Draw Mars to scale.
b. Draw Jupiter to scale.
c. How big is sun at this scale?

activity 13,17-18 A
Can you draw the solar system to scale on a sheet of notebook paper showing *both* the size of the planets and their distances from the sun? Explain.

activity 13,17-18 B
A star ship enters our solar system from deep space. How does the view change?

activity 15,16,18
Leo is lost in the sun about one month out of the year. Explain why.

activity 19 A
Optional: Sky Sphere.
Mars is in eastern quadrature. Where (if at all) do we see this planet...
a. After sunset?
b. At midnight?
c. Before sunrise?

activity 19 B
Optional: Sky Sphere.
Jupiter is in opposition. Where (if at all) do we see this planet...
a. After sunset?
b. At midnight?
c. Before sunrise?

activity 19 C
Optional: Sky Sphere.
Venus and Mercury are both at maximum Western elongation.
a. During what part of the night (between sunset and sunrise) do you see these planets?
b. Which planet do you see first? Why?

activity 20 A
Scorpius shines against the soft light of our Milky Way Galaxy. The square of Pegasus, by contrast, shines in inky darkness. Account for this difference.

activity 20 B
You broadcast your home address toward Andromeda, 2.2 million LY away, so that someday aliens from that galaxy might knock at your door and stay for dinner.
a. Detail your full address that you will broadcast, so these aliens will be able to locate you. Assume they can understand English.
b. How much time might pass before you could hope for their arrival? (Radio waves travel at the speed of light.)

activity 20 C
Optional: Kilometer Bar
Order by size from smallest to largest:
Sun's diameter
Earth's diameter
Earth's orbit
Jupiter's orbit
Pluto's orbit
across the Universe
distance to Alpha Centauri
distance to Mizar
distance to Alkaid
distance to Andromeda
Pluto's diameter
diameter of Milky Way
Jupiter

Answers (continued)

activity 10-12 A
a. one million = 1,000,000
b. ten trillion = 10,000,000,000,000
c. 10,000,000,000,000/1,000,000 = 10,000,000 sheets

activity 10-12 B
a. We would detect this solar flare on earth 8.3 minutes after it occurred: 500 sec x 1 min/60 sec = 8.3 min
b. distance to sun = 300,000 k/sec x 500 sec = 150,000,000 k
c. A sheet of newspaper contains 1 million Lots-o-Dots. If each dot is a token good for 1 kilometer, it takes 150 sheets of newspaper to travel this distance.

activity 12
a. 7 years
b. A 70 LY cube of space contains, 10 x 10 x 10 = 1,000 stars.
If the travel time from one star to another averaged 7 years, it would take 7,000 years to visit each star in this space.

activity 13
Students should mark off the distance between the sun and earth orbit (1 scale AU) on a piece of scrap paper, then use it as a ruler to place the other planets.

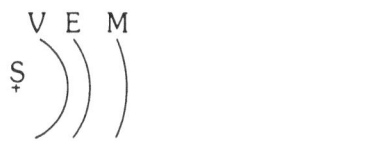

activity 13,18
This model shows how the planets are arranged, which ones are bigger, and which ones are smaller. But neither distance nor size is drawn to scale.

activity 14-16
a. Cassiopeia circles the NCP above my N horizon.
b. Orion rises in the east, culminates in the south, and sets in the west.
c. The Southern Cross circles up near my southern horizon but never rises above it.

activity 15-16 A
a. Students should draw any 4 of these:

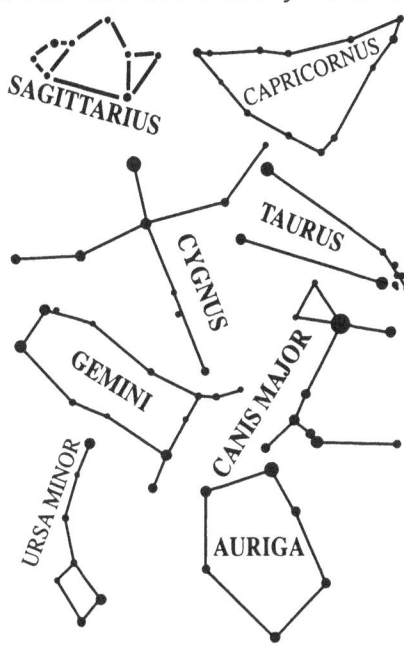

b. The zodiac constellations are Sagittarius, Capricornus, Taurus and Gemini.

activity 15-16 B
These constellations are (a) Aquila, (b) Bootes, (c) Cepheus, (d) Corona Borealis, (e) Ophiuchus, (f) Draco, (g) Perseus and (h) Corvus.

activity 16
Your meridian starts at the NCP, arcs through your zenith, and crosses your southern horizon.

activity 17
a. (Students should draw Mars equal to half a penny diameter – about 1 cm across.)
b. (Students should draw Jupiter equal to 11.2 penny diameters – about 22.4 cm across. This will run off the edge of a sheet of notebook paper.)
c. The sun equals 108 penny diameters at this scale.

activity 13,17-18 A
No. If the planets are drawn on a scale that is large enough to see, then their distances from the sun at this same scale are much too large to fit on a sheet of notebook paper.

activity 13,17-18 B
The view hardly changes at all. The sun is becoming a brighter and brighter star, but this was true before entering the solar system. The planets are still too small to stand out among the countless stars in the Milky Way. Your star ship must closely approach a planet before it appears any larger than a point of light.

activity 15,16,18
Earth's yearly orbit around the sun brings the sun into alignment with Leo once each year. For about 1 month out of the year it is too close to the sun to be seen before sunrise or after sunset.

activity 19 A
a. After sunset, Mars is culminating.
b. At midnight, Mars is setting in the west.
c. Mars is not visible at sunrise. It is somewhere below our feet.

activity 19 B
a. After sunset, Jupiter is rising in the east.
b. At midnight, Jupiter is culminating.
c. Before sunrise, Jupiter is setting in the west.

activity 19 C
a. At maximum Western elongation, Venus and Mercury both lead the sun, rising ahead of it in the morning before sunrise.
b. The larger orbit of Venus positions it farther west than Mercury. You see Venus first.

activity 20 A
From Earth we look toward the *center* of the galaxy to see Scorpius against a soft glowing background of billions of stars. We look *out* of the plane of the galaxy to see Pegasus against a black background with relatively few stars.

activity 20 B
a. My address: The Milky Way galaxy, in the solar system surrounding our star, the Sun, on the third planet out called Earth, on the North American continent, in (country), in (state or province), in (city), at (address).
b. It will take 2.2 million years for my message to arrive. Assuming it is heard and the invitation promptly accepted, it will take another 2.2 million years for these aliens to arrive at my door for dinner, assuming they can travel at the speed of light. So I'll have to wait a minimum of 4.4 million years, or much, much longer if they travel only as fast as Earthlings.

activity 20 C
From smallest to largest are: Pluto's diameter, Earth's diameter, Jupiter's diameter, Sun's diameter, Earth's orbit, Jupiter's orbit, Pluto's orbit, distance to Alpha Centauri, distance to Mizar, distance to Alkaid, diameter of Milky Way, distance to Andromeda, across the Universe.

ACTIVITIES
AND
LESSON NOTES
1-20

☞ As you distribute these duplicated worksheets, **please observe our copyright notice** at the front of this module. We allow you, the purchaser, to make as many copies as you need, but forbid supplying photocopied materials to other teachers for use in other classrooms.

☞ TOPS is a small, not-for-profit educational corporation, dedicated to making great science accessible to students everywhere. Our only income is from the sale of these inexpensive modules. If you would like to help spread the word that TOPS *is* tops, please request multiple copies of our free **TOPS Ideas** catalog to pass on to other educators or student teachers. These offer a variety of sample lessons, plus an order form for your colleagues to purchase their own TOPS modules. Thanks!

THE PLANETS AND THE STARS (   )1

LANDMARKS

1. Cut around the outside of the <u>Landmark</u> <u>Maps</u>, keeping them all in *one* piece.

a. Fold the maps like an accordion so CLASSROOM faces up.

b. Lightly stick them to a book on your desk, using masking tape.

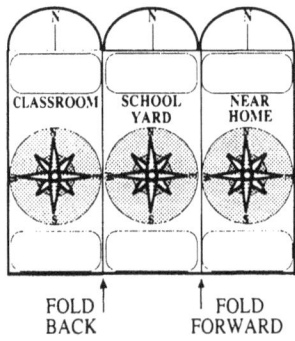

2. Turn the book so N on the *compass rose* points north, just like the meter stick hanging in your room.

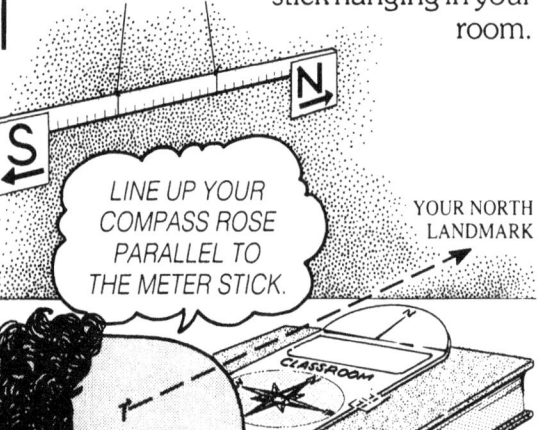

LINE UP YOUR COMPASS ROSE PARALLEL TO THE METER STICK.

YOUR NORTH LANDMARK

a. In the top curved section, draw a *distant* landmark that you now see to your north. (The "N" line should pass through the part of your drawing that is *exactly* north.)

b. Describe this landmark in words under your drawing.

c. Describe <u>your</u> position, in the box to the south of the compass rose.

d. Name something that is now due south of you; northwest of you; at a bearing of 60°.

e. Point your map toward its north landmark from other places in your room. Does your compass rose still agree with the meter stick? Explain.

3. The sun *culminates* (reaches its highest point in the sky) exactly halfway between sunrise and sunset. This is called *high noon*.

CULMINATION
HIGH NOON!
SUNRISE   SUNSET

a. Write down when the sun now rises and sets where you live.

b. Calculate when high noon happens where you live. Give your answer to the nearest minute.

4. If you live north of the Tropic of Cancer, the sun always passes directly to your south at high noon.

SUNLIGHT AT HIGH NOON

NORTH POLE
N
YOU ARE HERE
S
TROPIC OF CANCER
EQUATOR
TROPIC OF CAPRICORN

a. Where does your shadow point at high noon?

b. How can you use the sun and a clock to find true north outside?

5. Use the sun, if possible, to accurately complete the 2 remaining Landmark Maps.

LANDMARK
TRUE NORTH
A LOCATION YOU CAN FIND AGAIN

a. Choose a well-marked open place in the SCHOOL YARD that you can find again.

b. Find a safe place NEAR HOME with clear views to the N and S. It should be protected from bright street and house lights as much as possible.

Copyright © 1994 by TOPS Learning Systems, Canby OR 97013. Reproduction limited to personal classroom use.

Objective

To fix reference points that line up with true north in your classroom, on the school grounds and at home.

Supporting Concepts

The supporting concepts presented here, and throughout this module, may already be familiar to your students. Depending on the needs and abilities of your particular age group, you might decide to try all the ideas presented under these headings, cover a select few, or skip them entirely. The *less* you do and say by way of introduction, the *more* independent and self-directed your students will become.

✪ Call attention to the meter stick hanging in your classroom lettered N for north and S for south. These point toward earth's north and south poles. Ask everyone to point north, just like the meter stick. How can we describe the orientation of all our pointing fingers? (If everyone is pointing correctly, they are all parallel.)

✪ Ask volunteers to describe, in specific terms, something in the room that is due north of them. Does everyone describe the same object? (No. Different locations in the room have different North landmarks.)

Lesson Notes

2, 2a. Students tend to select prominent objects (a wall clock, for example) somewhere *near* true north, then draw these in the center of the available space. Encourage them to *first* align their maps parallel with the N-S meter stick, then accurately draw what they see as they sight along the N-line (not likely the exact center of the clock).

2c. Students should complete this activity at their "home" locations within the classroom. This might be at their desks if they work individually, or at an assigned lab table if teams of students share materials.

2d. Notice that this particular step and others in this lesson are underlined. These signal that a response is required on a separate assignment sheet or in a personal science notebook. (Steps 2a, 2b, and 2c are not underlined because students respond to instructions in these steps on their cutouts.)

3. This "peoplet" is standing in the Northern Hemisphere looking south toward the culminating sun, with east on the left, west on the right. South of the Tropic of Cancer (in Hawaii, for example) this illustration is not accurate near summer solstice, as the sun approaches an observer's zenith. In the tropics this picture is inaccurate most of the year. In Australia it is just plain wrong. Our point is this. If you live south of 23.5° N latitude (farther south than the tip of Florida), some adaptation of these lesson materials will be necessary. If you live farther south than this, even more adaptation is required. This is an unfortunate limitation of basic geometry. Wherever you do live, however, you will find this module is still a marvelous astronomy resource.

5. If you can begin this activity about 1/2 hour before high noon, then the sun will culminate just as your students reach this step. If your schedule lacks this flexibility, predetermine a suitable placed on your school grounds and locate its N landmark in advance for students to copy. Use your own sun shadow to do this, or a magnetic compass corrected to true north.

5a. You may wish to discuss suitable SCHOOL YARD viewing sites before going outside:

• The site should be easy to recognize and remember.
• It should have plenty of open sky to the north and south.
• The site's north horizon should be as distant as possible. (If you are able to select a N landmark that is many miles away on your far horizon, then this single landmark will serve as a N reference from anywhere in your whole school yard.)

5b. This is an important homework assignment that lays the groundwork for successful night sky viewing NEAR HOME later on. All of the criteria in 5a apply, as well as issues of darkness and safety.

Though not specifically directed to do so, your students should identify these Landmark Maps (and all cutouts in this module) with their names. They should save these maps (and all future cutouts) to use in later activities.

Answers

2d. Students should describe classroom objects at each compass point. All answers are unique to each site.

2e. No. When you point the map at its north landmark from other places in the room, N and S on the compass rose no longer align (point parallel) to N and S on the meter stick. (The only exception to this is if you move to a new location directly north or south of your original location. Then your north landmark remains unchanged.)

3a. Students should copy the sunrise and sunset times that you wrote on the blackboard.

3b. An easy way to solve this problem is to add and subtract time in equal increments from sunrise and sunset times until you zero in on high noon. Here is a daylight savings time example:

sunrise = 7:20	sunset = 6:34
+ 6 hr = 1:20	- 6 hr = 12:34
- 20 min = 1:00	+ 20 min = 12:54
- 3 min = 12:57	+3 min = 12:57 (high noon)

(Our clocks keep average solar time. The sun will run ahead or lag behind any high noon you calculate as the year progresses.)

4a. At high noon your shadow always points directly north.

4b. Keep an appointment with the culminating sun. When it is high noon by your calculations in 3b, go outside and observe your sun shadow. It points true north.

✓ Landmark Maps: Are all 3 spaces on all 3 maps complete? Is each student's classroom site at a suitable location for conducting future experiments?

Materials

☐ The Landmark Maps cutout. Find photocopy masters for this and all cutouts at the back of this book.
☐ Scissors and masking tape.
☐ A heavy textbook.
☐ A level work area. This might be a desk or lab table.
☐ A meter stick labeled "N" and "S." (See the illustration in step 2.) Suspend this from your ceiling with string in the correct orientation. To find north, observe the direction of shadows outside your window at high noon, or use a compass.
☐ List the rising and setting times of the sun on your blackboard. These depend on your latitude and time of year. They are often listed in the weather section of local newspapers. You can also calculate these times from a current almanac, or use direct observation.
☐ A clock or wrist watch.

POINTER BOX

THE PLANETS AND THE STARS ( )2

A. Complete steps 1-11 **in order**.

1. Carefully cut out the Earth Circle. Poke a pinhole precisely through the dot that marks your home latitude. Do this on *both* sides of the North Pole.

2. Seal an empty cereal box shut with masking tape. Fold your Landmark Maps with CLASSROOM on top. Lightly tape it to the box top where marked, and fold the north "window" upright.

3. Aim the north "window" on your box toward your north landmark. Hold your Earth Circle against the upper south corner, on the side of your box that is easiest to reach. (Your upper south corner *might* be on the right — we've drawn it on the left.)

4. Rotate the circle so its North Pole leans toward the box's north "window." Put a pin into the latitude pinhole that comes to the top, but not into the box.

5. While the Earth Circle hangs on the pin, position it to just meet the top and south edges of your box. Stick the pin into the box at this position. (You can pad your thumb with a penny.)

6. Swing the Earth Circle on the pin to be sure it rests perfectly framed in the upper south corner of the box. Tape around its edge to secure its position when it stops swinging.

7. Remove the pin. Draw yourself as a small stick figure standing at your latitude on "top" of the world with arms outstretched. Label it "home."

8. Stick 2 pieces of clear tape along the end of a straw to make at "roof:"

Press this end of the straw onto your paper "earth" precisely over the straw pattern, so its extra length points downward.

9. Cut off the straw just beyond the box. Join the cut-off part to another whole straw with a paper clip opened halfway like a book.

10. Adjust the paper clip "elbow" so the straws match this right angle.

11. Slice open the *short* straw almost to the paper-clip elbow. Push this sliced end into the taped straw like a "bent arm" into a sleeve.

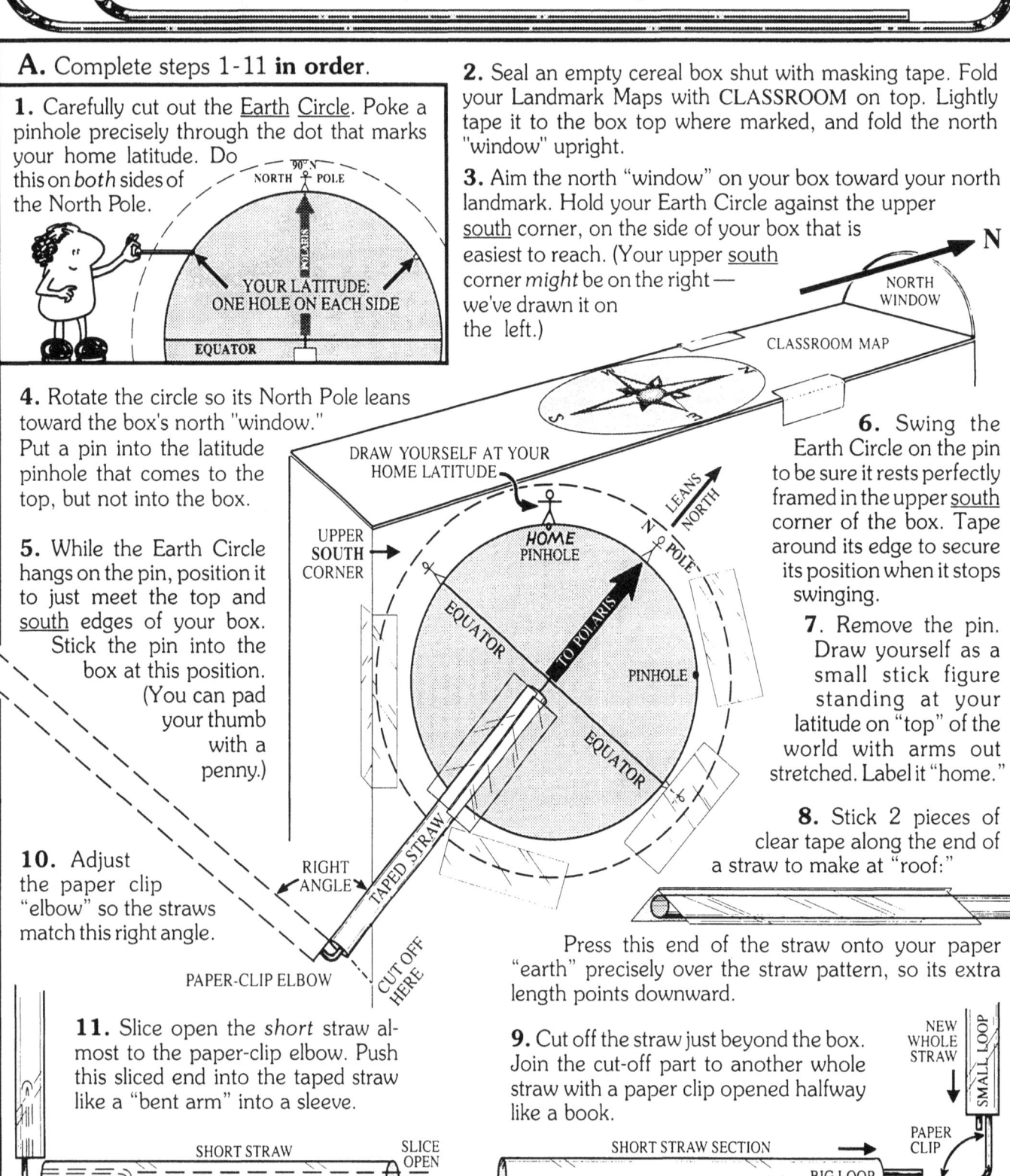

B. Cut out the Concept List for this activity. Work through the numbers (in order) with a friend.

1. Take turns reading each concept aloud, then demonstrate (on the Pointer Box) that it is true.

2. Circle each concept number that you *both* understand. How many numbers did you circle?

Copyright © 1994 by TOPS Learning Systems, Canby OR 97013. Reproduction limited to personal classroom use.

Objective

To construct a Pointer Box to determine the locations of Polaris and the celestial equator at your latitude.

Lesson Notes

2. Stick the Landmark Maps to the cereal box with masking tape. As students need to fold other maps on top, they can peel back the masking tape and reuse it.

3-5. This Pointer Box illustration corresponds to the actual view of a student facing west. It is a mirror image of what east-facing students will build: their Pointer Boxes will have the Earth Circle on the opposite side of the box. Students who read the directions will not be confused; those who look only at the illustration may need assistance.

6-7. If the Earth Circle is allowed to swing freely, gravity will bring it to rest with your home latitude on top. This models how observers at any latitude see their world, as if they were standing on top of it.

8. Younger students may need help in this step. If the straw doesn't sit squarely on its pattern, gently lift it free and start over with fresh tape. Once it is accurately placed, press in the tape "roof" along both sides to minimize the gap between the paper and straw. A paper clip makes a convenient pushing tool.

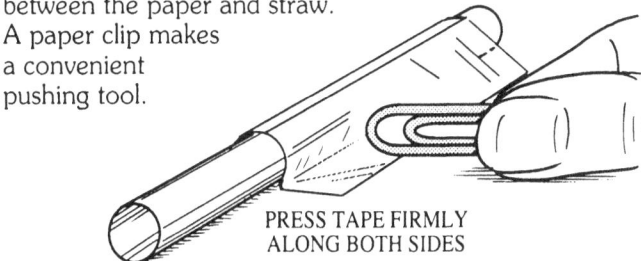

PRESS TAPE FIRMLY ALONG BOTH SIDES

If the straw rolls off its pattern, simply twist it in the opposite direction to recenter.

9. Notice that the big loop fits into the short straw while the small loop fits into the long one. A reverse fit also works, though not quite as well.

Bend either loop as necessary to fit snugly: To narrow the large loop, bend it closed, then reopen; to widen the small loop, spread it just a little.

B. Concept List (Guide to Oral Discussion):

This concept lists (and all others in this module) offer great opportunities to learn kinesthetically and solve problems cooperatively. Complete mastery is not the goal; rather, intellectual growth and increasing self confidence.

1. My *zenith* is always straight overhead. My home stick figure on top of the Earth Circle sees the same stars at its zenith that I do at my zenith: *Straight up for me is in the same direction as straight up for my home figure. We both see the same stars overhead.*

2. The zeniths of all four stick figures are directed outward from the earth's center, like spokes in a wheel: *Students might finger-trace a straight line out from the center of the earth toward the zenith of each stick figure.*

3. My home figure's outstretched arms point N and S: *The compass rose on the box top confirms this.*

4. If the home figure travels N, it eventually reaches the north pole. If it travels S, it eventually reaches the equator: *Students should finger-trace the journeys of their home figures moving north or south along the curve of the earth.*

5. My outstretched arms trace my *horizon* as I turn in a circle. I share the same horizon with my home figure on top of the Earth Circle: *My home figure's outstretched arms and my own arms are both horizontal, pointing to a common horizon.*

6. The arrow labeled "To Polaris" on the Earth Circle points into the sky above the N horizon of my home figure. This is where my home figure sees Polaris, a star in the night sky: *Students should observe that the Polaris arrow leans toward the N end of the compass rose.*

7. Polaris is at the zenith of the north pole figure, and at the N horizon of both equator figures: *The Polaris Straw points straight over the north-pole figure's head; it points parallel to the equator figures' horizon-pointing arms.*

8. The long straw rotates east and west through my home figure's southern sky. This traces out its *celestial equator*: *Students should sweep the long straw as indicated.*

9. In March and September the sun appears to move along my *celestial equator*. During these times, it rises east of my compass rose, culminates over my southern horizon, and sets west of my compass rose: *Students should line up the N window on their Pointer Boxes with their N landmarks, then sweep the long straw from east to west through their southerly sky.*

10. The celestial equator circles the horizon of the north pole figure; it crosses the zeniths of the equator figures: *The long straw sweeps parallel to the north pole figure's outstretched arms and the equator figures' vertical bodies.*

11. When you fly around the earth's equator, the celestial equator is always straight over your head: *The long straw sweeps through a circle that is always straight out from the earth's equator.*

12. The numbers under my home figure's feet (earth latitudes) always equal the numbers over its head (sky declinations). This is true wherever it walks: *The inner latitude numbers and outer declination numbers match at all locations around the earth.*

Answers

B2. Students should count the total number of concepts they understand and write that number. This is the only written response in this activity.

✓ Pointer Box: Is the Earth Circle securely fixed in the upper south corner of the box, home latitude on top? Is the straw accurately taped over its pattern? Does the long straw turn freely? Does the paper clip elbow join both straws at a right angle? (This right angle orientation is assumed in step 3a of the next activity.)

Materials

H Write your home latitude on the blackboard to the nearest degree. Consult an almanac to find the latitude of a major city nearest you. Add 1° for every 69 miles that you are north of this reference city; subtract 1° for every 69 miles south. You can also estimate your latitude using a world globe.

☐ The Earth Circle cutout.
☐ Scissors.
☐ A straight pin.
☐ Landmarks Maps from the previous activity.
☐ Masking tape.
☐ A 32 ounce Grape-Nuts box. This brand is recommended for sturdy construction and ideal size. The Landmark Maps won't fit smaller boxes, but you can substitute larger cereal boxes and center the maps inside the extra space on top of the box. A second cereal box is needed to model the Big Dipper in activity 7. Gather 2 boxes per activity group if students are sharing materials, or 2 boxes per student if they are working independently.
☐ A penny.
☐ Clear tape.
☐ Standard-sized paper clips.
☐ Straight plastic straws about 1/4 inch in diameter or slightly smaller. Make sure these fit your paper clips. See note 9 above.

THE PLANETS AND THE STARS (   )3

SUN DECLINATIONS

1. Cut around the Sun Protractor. Punch out the black spot.

2. Get your Pointer Box. Line up its N window with your north landmark.

3. Hold your Sun Protractor against the bent "arm" on your Pointer Box. Align both black arrows (labeled "To Polaris") while the paper clip "elbow" remains centered behind the hole.

a. To what *declination* (degrees on the protractor) does the Sun Straw now point?

b. The Sun Straw points to the sun at this declination on about the 21st of what month(s)? What do we call this special day (or days)?

c. Track the "sun" through a "day" with your Sun Straw, from level horizon to level horizon. According to your compass rose, in what direction is the sunrise; the sunset?

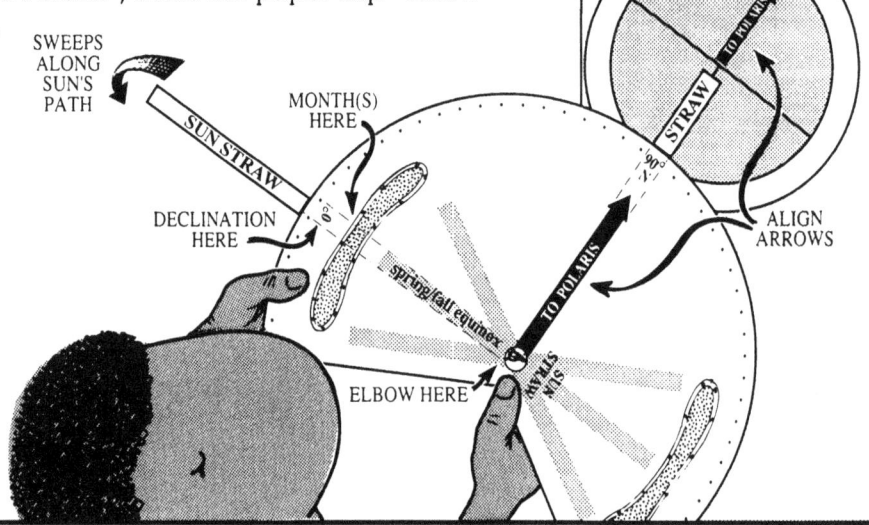

4. Bend the paper-clip elbow (never the straw) upward to the summer solstice position. (Always slide the "bent arm" off before adjusting the elbow.) Repeat step 3 for this new position, answering parts a, b and c.

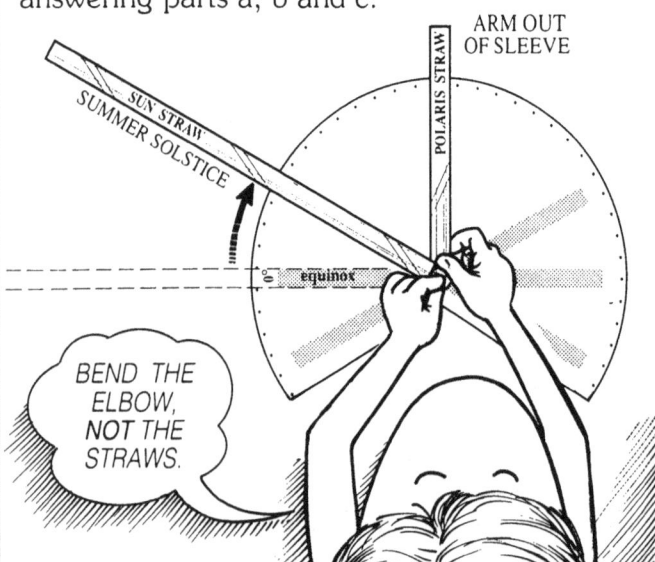

BEND THE ELBOW, NOT THE STRAWS.

5. Bend the paper clip elbow downward to its winter solstice position. Repeat step 3 for this new position, answering parts a, b and c.

6. Copy this table and fill it in. Include a final entry for today's date.

DATE IN CALENDAR YEAR	DECLINATION	WHERE THE SUN RISES	SETS
Winter Solstice (*Dec 21*)			
Spring Equinox (*Mar 21*)			
Summer Solstice (*Jun 21*)			
Fall Equinox (*Sep 21*)			
TODAY (*current date*)			

Lightly tape the Sun Protractor to the unused side of your Pointer Box for storage.

Copyright © 1994 by TOPS Learning Systems, Canby OR 97013. Reproduction limited to personal classroom use.

Objective

To trace the path of the sun across the sky at its solstice and equinox positions. To observe where the sun rises and sets during different times of the year.

Supporting Concepts

⊙ Lightly tape the Sun Protractor to a Pointer Box with the straws set at a right angle as shown in step 3. Turn it so the compass rose is properly oriented. Ask questions like these to ease younger students into a comfortable relationship with their Sun Protractors.

• To what declination does the Polaris Straw point? (90° N)
• To what declination does the long Sun Straw point? (0°)
• At what declination is the celestial equator? (0°)
• On what special days is the sun at the celestial equator? (spring equinox and fall equinox)
• During what calendar months is the sun in the equinox positions? (September and March on the month loops.)
• What is the declination of your zenith? (your latitude)
• What is the declination of your horizon? (90° N minus your latitude)
• Are the declinations around the Earth Circle equal to the numbers on your protractor? (Yes. They correspond all the way around.)
• Is a declination a point or a line? (It is a complete circle, swept out by the Sun Straw on the Pointer Box. Bend this straw at different angles to sweep out different declination circles.)

⊙ If you have a world globe, consider this demonstration:

• Use your hands to pantomime the *celestial sphere* (our dome-shaped sky) several centimeters above the globe.
• Reach through this celestial sphere to finger-trace the *earth's equator*, maintaining contact with the globe's surface all the way around. Now trace around the *celestial equator*, by repeating the same circle. This time keep your finger several centimeters above the earth's equator on your imaginary celestial sphere. Notice that both equators perfectly match all the way around.

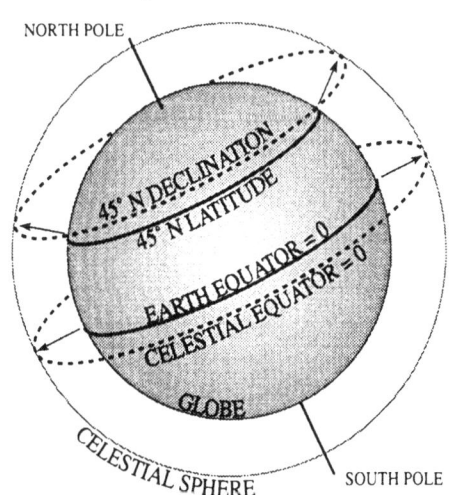

• Repeat for other latitude circles on the globe, N or S of the equator. The earth and sky are divided by matching grid systems. Circles of latitude always match circles of declination.

Lesson Notes

3. In step 10 of the previous activity, both straws were set at a right angle. This must be their alignment now, to point to a declination of 0°.

6. To set the straws at today's date, find it on the Sun Protractor's month loop. Mark that date for younger students, then set both straws at the corresponding angle. Bend only the paper clip elbow, never the straws.

Answers

3a. The Sun Straw now points to a declination of 0°.
3b. The sun is at 0° around the 21st of March and September. These special days are called the spring equinox and fall equinox.
3c. During spring and fall equinox, the sun rises due east of the compass rose and sets due west.
4a. The Sun Straw now points to a declination of 22.5° N.
4b. The sun is at 22.5° N on about the 21st of June. This special day is called the summer solstice.
4c. During summer solstice, the sun rises *north* of due east and sets *north* of due west.
5a. The Sun Straw now points to a declination of 22.5° S.
5b. The sun is at 22.5° S on about the 21st of December. This special day is called the winter solstice.
5c. During winter solstice, the sun rises *south* of due east and sets *south* of due west.
6. This table requires your students to summarize all the sun information they have gathered so far in a table. Some may simply copy what they have already written. Others will repeat the experiment. Either way, they'll solidify important concepts.

The bottom line of this table does break new ground. Students should bend the paper clip elbow so it corresponds to their current position in the month loop. You can help students who have difficulty here, by identifying that calendar position in the loop with a pencil mark.

DATE IN CALENDAR YEAR	DECLINATION	WHERE THE SUN RISES	SETS
Winter Solstice (*Dec 21*)	23.5° N	S of E	S of W
Spring Equinox (*Mar 21*)	0°	due E	due W
Summer Solstice (*Jun 21*)	23.5° S	N of E	N of W
Fall Equinox (*Sep 21*)	0°	due E	due W
TODAY (*current date*)			

Materials

☐ The Sun Protractor cutout.
☐ Scissors.
☐ A paper punch tool.
☐ The Pointer Box.
☐ Masking tape.

THE PLANETS AND THE STARS ( )4

FOLLOW THAT STAR

1. Cut out the <u>Shadow Screen</u>. Punch out the black center spot.

a. Cover the hole (one side only) with clear tape. Shred it in many directions with a pin.

b. Slide the "bent arm" out of its sleeve. Gently insert the long Sun Straw through the shredded-tape hole, and slide the Shadow Screen about halfway down.

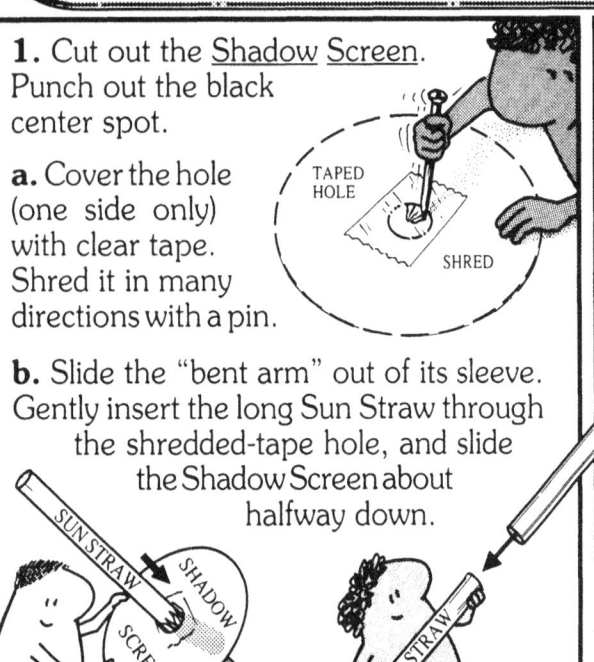

2. Hold the Sun Straw up to direct sunlight so it casts a shadow across the screen.

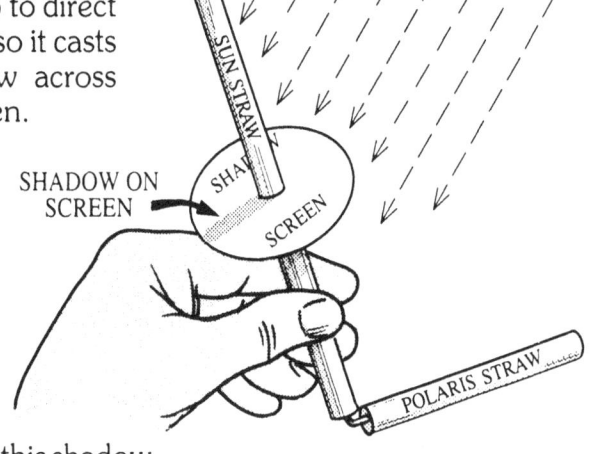

a. Make this shadow smaller and smaller until it disappears. Where is the sun in relation to this straw?

b. If your body casts the shortest possible sun shadow, where is the sun?

CAUTION: protect your eyes: *Never* look directly into the sun.

3. Use your Sun Protractor to check that the Sun Straw is correctly angled for today's sun declination. (Slide it out of the sleeve if you need to bend the elbow.)

a. Change the Landmark Maps on the box top so SCHOOL YARD faces up. When you retape it in place, make sure the Polaris Straw correctly leans toward the N landmark window.

b. Tie a thread to a washer. Explain how to use this plumb line to make sure your box rests level on bumpy ground.

4. Go to your school yard site when the sun is shining. Line up your Pointer Box with its N landmark. If it's windy, place rocks inside (or around the base) for ballast.
a. Use your plumb line to be sure that the box is level.
b. Verify that your sweeper straw really does point to the sun at today's declination. (Track the sun, throughout the day if possible, without moving the box.)
c. Write a report.

Objective

To verify that the Sun Straw on the Pointer Box really tracks the apparent path of the sun across the sky.

Supporting Concepts

✪ The Sun Straw on your Pointer Box tracks our sun, as well as distant "suns," across our sky. Here's how to track the path of Sirius, the brightest star in our night sky. It has a declination of 17° S.

• Slide the bent straw arm out of its sleeve, and lay the Polaris Straw on top of the black arrow of the Sun Protractor. Bend the paper clip elbow so the Sun Straw points to 17° S.

• Insert these straws back into the Pointer Box. Turn the box so its N window matches its N landmark.

• Sweep the Sun Straw from east to west to trace the path of Sirius across your classroom walls and ceiling.

✪ Because the earth rotates on its axis, Sirius appears to move in a full 360° circle about once a day.

• Turn the Polaris Straw 90° at a time (quarter-turn increments) to track the star's motion over quarter-day intervals.

• Turn the Polaris Straw 45° at a time (eighth-turn increments) to track the star's motion over 3 hour intervals.

Lesson Notes

1a-b. If the Shadow Screen is pushed down on the straw from above as illustrated, then its shredded sticky "fingers" will "grab" the straw as it slides. If your straw's diameter is somewhat smaller than the paper punch hole, this will help hold the Shadow Screen in place. If your straw's diameter is nearly as large as the hole, however, its is better to push the straw up from the bottom so only the slippery side of the tape "fingers" make contact.

3. This is only a checking step. The straw's arm has most likely *already* been bent to today's declination from the previous activity. If it needs further adjustment, students may need to temporarily remove the shadow screen.

4. Place large rocks or bricks against the base of the box to stabilize it from the outside. Add a cup or two of gravel as inside ballast.

Answers

2a. When the shadow fully disappears, the straw is aimed directly at the sun.

2b. The sun culminates at its highest point in the sky when your body casts its shortest possible sun shadow.

3b. Hold the plumb line near any of its 4 upper corners. If the Pointer Box is level, then the edge will be vertical, running parallel to the plumb line.

4c. Sample report: I took the Pointer Box to my school yard site on a sunny day. Because it was windy, I filled the box about 1/5 full of gravel so it wouldn't blow over. Then I lined up its N window with my N landmark and used a plumb line to check that the box was vertical. Being careful not to move the box, I gently swept the Sun Straw, set at today's declination, from east to west. I stopped it where the straw's shadow completely disappeared. In this position it pointed directly at the sun. I returned every hour or so and nudged it westward to where the shadow disappeared again. In this manner, the Sun Straw tracked the sun's position throughout the day, fixing its culminating, setting and rising positions.

Extension

Q. The Big Dipper has a declination of about 55° N. Track this familiar pattern of stars, through a day and a night, across the walls and ceiling of your classroom. You'll need to invent a way to allow the rotating Sun Straw to freely turn through a complete circle.

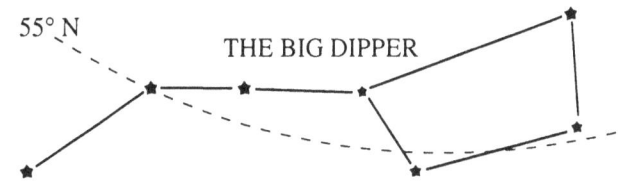

A. Set the angle between the straws on your Pointer Box to 55° N as measured by the Sun Protractor. Extend the Polaris Straw with another full-length straw, slit in the end to facilitate joining. Slide the box to the edge of your table so the Sun Straw hangs beyond the edge. In this position, with the Polaris Straw aimed at Polaris, the Sun Straw sweeps out the full path of the Big Dipper around Polaris.)

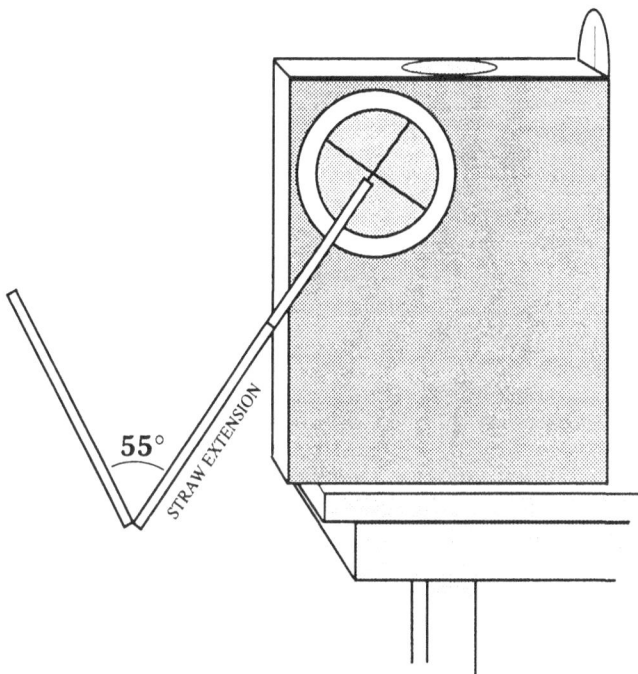

Materials

☐ The Shadow Screen cutout.
☐ Scissors.
☐ A paper punch tool.
☐ Clear tape.
☐ A straight pin.
☐ The Pointer Box and Sun Protractor from the previous activity.
☐ A sunny day. If the day is not clear enough to see distinct shadows, skip ahead to the next activity and return when the sun is shining. If sunny days are rare, substitute a flashlight in step 2, or any other light source that throws a shadow on paper, then continue on through step 4b. Your students might even write up the report in 4c along these lines: If the sun *were* shining, then with the Pointer Box properly aligned, the Sun Straw *would have* swung through a position where the sun cast no shadow...
☐ A spool of thread.
☐ A washer.
☐ Gravel, large rocks or bricks (optional).

THE PLANETS AND THE STARS ( )5

EARTH IN A JAR

1. Find the volume (in milliliters) of a small jar filled to the brim with water.
a. What is half this volume?
b. Make a pencil mark on a small piece of tape to show how high this much water reaches.
c. Empty and dry the jar.

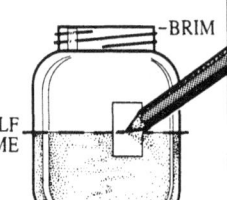

2. Cut out all 4 Long Maps. Keep that strip that best matches the circumference of your jar. Discard the rest.
a. Name the 4 *constellations* on this strip, the month line, and the hour line.
b. Boldly trace these constellations and lines on the back of this strip against a window. (Don't trace words or numbers.)
c. Carefully trim away all extra white paper. Don't cut into lines or words.

Just Right!

3. Cut *inside* the dashed line of the Short Map, to remove extra white paper. Window-trace both constellations, plus a dot for the star Polaris.

4. Tape the Long Map around the jar like an upside-down belt with the printed side facing out. The celestial equator should meet full circle on your pencil mark.

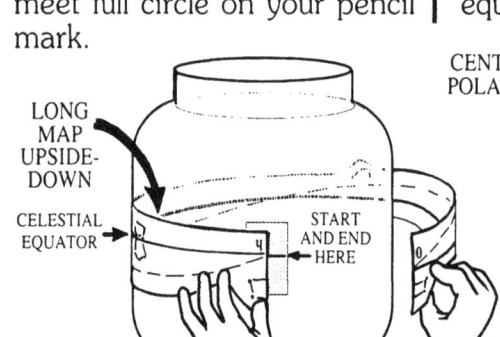

5. Set the Short Map (printed side up) on the glass bottom. Center Polaris and position the last star in the Big Dipper handle over the tiny x on the celestial equator (near 14 h). Tape in place.

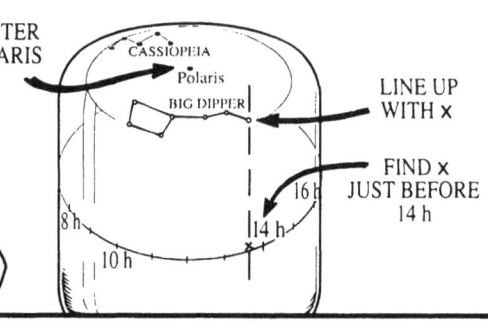

6. Follow these directions *in order* from **a** to **f**.

START HERE ↓

f. Stick a small clay "sun" on the jar's ecliptic circle over your current date.

a. Open a paper clip halfway, like a book. Straighten the large loop into a "pole," and spread the small loop into a wide "foot."

e. Set the jar on top. Adjust the clay "earth," if necessary, so it "floats" in the center of your Star Jar.

d. Punch out the tiny Compass Circle. Pin it about halfway between the equator and north pole so N is up.

c. Roll a clay "earth" about this big. Stick it over the wire to form a "north pole." Scrape an "equator" around its middle with a pin. ▲

b. Center the pole *inside* the lid. Secure its foot with crossed strips of masking tape. (Poke the pole through one strip.)

7. Get the Concept List for this activity. Work through the numbers (in order) with a friend.
a. Take turns reading each concept aloud, then demonstrating (on the Star Jar) that it is true.
b. Circle each concept number that you *both* understand. How many numbers did you circle?

Objective

To construct a mini-planetarium in a baby food jar. To model the apparent motion of the sun and stars around our rotating earth.

Lesson Notes

2. Different brands of 4-ounce baby food jars have slightly different circumferences depending on their brand and date of manufacture. These 4 Long Maps anticipate the range of these differences. Make sure your particular jars fit at least one of these maps with minimum gaps or overlaps. Enlarge or reduce these patterns, if necessary, to insure a good fit.

2-3. It is important to cut away as much excess paper as possible to open up the widest possible views.

4-5. These constellations may be taped or glued to the glass. The directions call for tape because it is easiest to handle. To preserve the maximum possible area for clear viewing, make sure your students use only small pieces of tape and apply them sparingly. Glue makes a more attractive and permanent presentation without covering additional glass. If your students are able to use it carefully, replace the verb "Tape" in each step with the word "Glue."

6b. Apply one strip of tape across the width of the "foot". To eliminate corner gaps, first press it firmly across the bottom and into the corners of the lid, then up its sides and over the lip. Spindle a second strip over the paper clip pole and apply it perpendicular to the first in the same manner.

6c. To start and end the equator in the same place, hold the pin stationary while turning the ball full circle on the paper clip, as if it were on a lathe.

7. Concept List (Guide to Oral Discussion):

1. Tilt the jar so the "pin person" stands straight up on "top" of the earth, surrounded by the stars and sun. This models how I'm standing on "top" of the real world: *Students should hold the jar as described and notice they have the same vertical orientation as the "pin person."*

2. Turn the clay "sun" to high noon over the pin person. This shows that the sun is *not* straight over my head; it is to my south: *Hold the lid still with the pin person on top, while turning the jar until the clay sun also comes to the top. In this position, the sun remains somewhat south of the pin person.*

3. Earth view: I seem to stand still while the sun and stars move *westward* across my sky: *Hold the lid still with the pin person on top while turning the jar from east to west across the pin person's compass circle.*

4. Space view: The earth rotates *eastward* while the sun and stars stand still: *Hold the jar still while turning the lid so east on the compass circle leads and west follows in a circle.*

5. You can model how the sun and stars move by turning the jar westward or turning the lid eastward. Either way, the pin person "sees" the same motion: *Turning the jar models the apparent motion of the sun and stars as seen by an earth observer. Turning the lid models the earth's actual rotation in space which produces this apparent motion. Either way, the sun and stars pass over the surface of the earth in the same direction.*

6. The clay sun appears to move full circle through the fixed background stars once a year. Tiny "suns" mark its position on the ecliptic circle at the beginning of each month: *Students should move the clay marker from one sun symbol to the next, moving full circle around the Star Jar.*

7. The *celestial equator* is located directly above the earth's equator. It is divided into 24 star hours: *Students should confirm that the equators are lined up one above the other; that the celestial equator is divided into 24 parts.*

8. The sun appears farthest north of the celestial equator about June 21st (summer solstice). It appears farthest south about December 21st (winter solstice): *Students should notice that the ecliptic circle reaches its widest separation north or south of the celestial equator at these dates.*

9. I seem to stand still while the sun and stars move in circles around the North Celestial Pole (NCP). Polaris, over my north horizon, is the only star that seems not to move: *Students should turn the jar westward, while holding the pin person in an upright position. All the stars and constellations appear to pivot around the NCP located above the pin person's north horizon. Because Polaris circles so close to this point, it appears stationary in the pin person's north sky.*

10. The Big Dipper appears to circle counterclockwise in my northern sky. This circle extends from overhead to horizon: *As students turn their Star Jars westward over the stationary pin person, they will observer that the Big Dipper moves as described in the pin person's north sky.*

11. Set your clay "sun" over the fall equinox position at 12h. At that time of year Scorpius culminates near sunset; Pegasus culminates near midnight; Orion culminates near sunrise; Leo culminates near noon: *When the clay "sun" is fixed among the stars at 12h, each constellation culminates in the order stated as the sun moves through its sunset, midnight, sunrise and noon positions.*

12. Set your clay sun over the spring equinox position at 0h. At that time of year, Orion culminates near sunset; Leo culminates near midnight; Scorpius culminates near sunrise; Pegasus culminates near noon: *When the clay "sun" is fixed among the stars at 0h, each constellation culminates in the order stated as the sun moves through its sunset, midnight, sunrise and noon positions.*

Answers

1. Our particular 4 ounce jar held 126 ml when filled to the brim with water. Your jars should hold a similar volume.
1a. 126 ml / 2 = 63 ml.

2a. The 4 constellations are called Pegasus, Orion, Leo and Scorpius. The month line is called the ecliptic circle. The hour line is called the celestial equator.

7b. Students should count the total number of concepts they understand and write that number.

✓ Star Jar (with clay earth): Is the Celestial Equator centered over Earth's equator? Is Polaris centered on the glass bottom with the cup of the Big Dipper over Leo? Are both maps traced and trimmed? Does the pin point straight out from the clay earth's center? Does N on the Compass Circle point to the earth's N pole?

Materials

☐ A 4 oz. baby food jar with a tight fitting lid. Select basic cylindrical shapes. Avoid unusual shapes. See note 2.
☐ A 50 ml graduated cylinder (optional). You can get by without it using this trick: Fill your jar brim full, then pour just enough of its water into an identical jar so the water levels match. Each will then be half full.
☐ A source of water and a towel.
☐ Clear tape. Or substitute white glue. See note 4-5.
☐ The cutout for this activity that includes the Long Maps, Short Map and Compass Circle.
☐ Scissors.
☐ A window or light table suitable for making tracings.
☐ A paper clip.
☐ Masking tape.
☐ Modeling clay.
☐ A straight pin.
☐ A paper punch tool.
☐ The Concept List cutout for this activity.

THE PLANETS AND THE STARS ( )6
OCEAN IN A JAR

1. Align your Pointer Box with its CLASSROOM landmark. Adjust the Sun Straw to track the path of the sun during the spring or fall equinox.

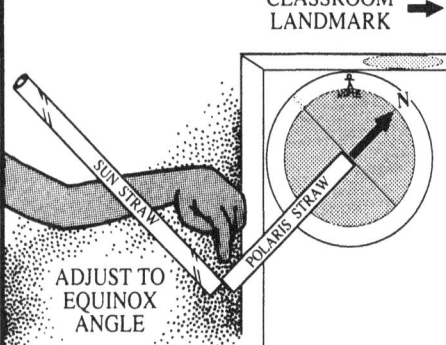

a. Where is Polaris in your sky?
b. Trace the path of the equinox sun across your sky from sunrise to sunset.

2. Tilt your Pointer Box up on one edge so the Equator person stands on "top" of the world.

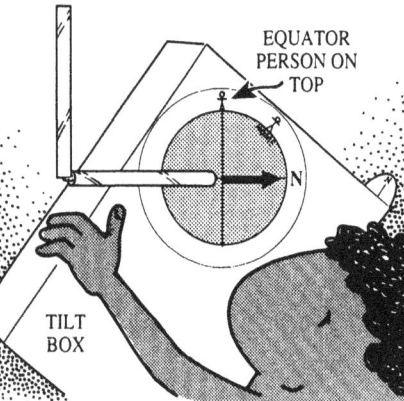

a. Where is Polaris for the equator person?
b. Trace the path of the equinox sun across the equatorial sky from sunrise to sunset.

3. Tilt your Pointer Box up on its other edge so the North Pole person stands on "top" of the world.

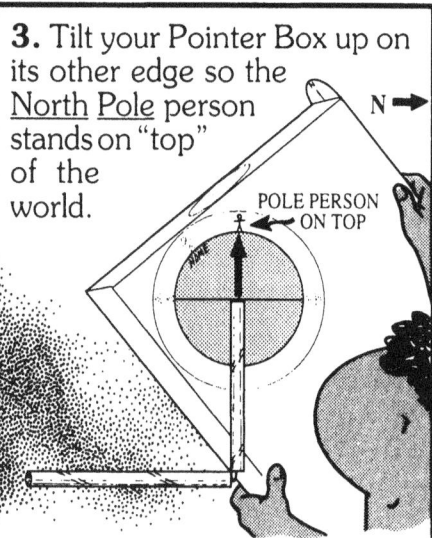

a. Where is Polaris for the north pole person?
b. Trace the path of the equinox sun across the polar sky from sunrise to sunset.

4. Add water to your Star Jar up to the Celestial Equator. Add a drop of food coloring, then cover with a square of plastic wrap.
a. Remove the clay "earth" and paper clip from the Star Jar's lid. Find which Round Map fits the lid. Cut it out.
b. Fold the tabs. Tape them around the outside of the lid.
c. Find the white "star" in the Southern Cross. Close the jar so this star lines up over the tiny **y** on the celestial equator (near 12 h).
d. Push on the lid with all your weight to tightly seal the jar. (When you shake it, no water should leak out.)
e. Trim away excess plastic wrap.

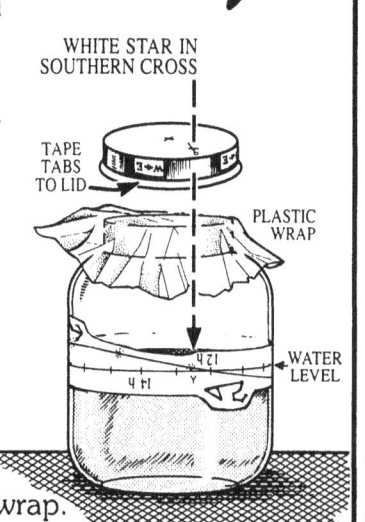

5. Point Polaris on your Star Jar to its actual location in your sky, while turning the jar from E to W (as marked on the lid).
a. Look inside the jar to watch Pegasus, Orion, Leo and Scorpius rise and set at your "ocean horizon."

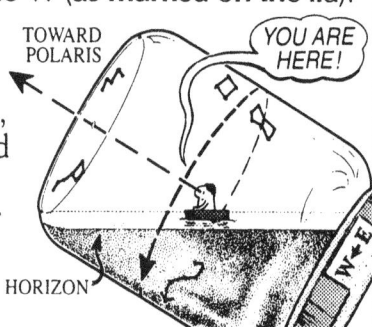

b. Which arrow best describes the motion of these constellations near your horizon?

PERPENDICULAR MOVEMENT — PARALLEL MOVEMENT — MOVEMENT AT AN ANGLE

6. Point Polaris on your jar to where you would see it if standing at the equator: repeat steps 5a and 5b.

7. Point Polaris on your jar to where you would see it if standing at the north pole: repeat steps 5a and 5b.

8. Cut out the Concept Table for this activity. Take turns reading each number aloud, then demonstrating each event at all 3 positions with your Star Jar. How many numbers did you both understand?

Copyright © 1994 by TOPS Learning Systems, Canby OR 97013. Reproduction limited to personal classroom use.

Objective

To model how the sun and stars move relative to a flat horizon. To compare this motion at different latitudes.

Lesson Notes

1. This direction assumes that your students are by now familiar with Pointer Box setup procedures:
 • Refold the landmark maps, CLASSROOM up, and retape so the Polaris Straw points toward the N Window.
 • Line up the N window with the N landmark.
 • Bend the straws to a right angle at the paper clip elbow using the Sun Protractor as a guide.

1-3. The activity sheet shows Pointer Boxes that were made while facing west. Those shown below were constructed while facing east.

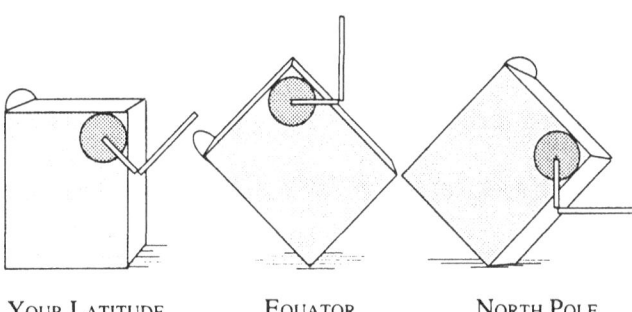

YOUR LATITUDE   EQUATOR   NORTH POLE

4b. If your students glued the constellations to the glass, they should glue this Round Map on as well. Substitute "Glue" for "Tape" in the second sentence.

4d. The lid must not leak. If necessary, *carefully* step on the jar and lid with your shoe. (Don't let your students try this.)

5-7. To answer these questions, point Polaris on the bottom of the Star Jar in the same direction the Polaris Straw points at each latitude.

8. <u>Concept List (Guide to Oral Discussion)</u>:
 You can demonstrate all 18 events in this concept table by aiming the glass bottom of the Star Jar north <u>and</u> rotating it in the direction of the lid arrows. As you do this...

Hold the jar <u>horizontally</u> for this column.	Tilt the jar like <u>the Polaris Straw</u> for this column.	Hold the jar <u>vertically</u> for this column.
1. Polaris appears fixed *on* my N horizon.	1. Polaris appears fixed *above* my N horizon.	1. Polaris appears fixed at my zenith.
2. Cassiopeia rises in the NE and sets in the NW.	2. Cassiopeia dips low to my N horizon and rises overhead.	2. Cassiopeia circles around my zenith.
3. Orion rises in the east, culminates at my zenith, and sets in the west.	3. Orion rises in the east, culminates to my south, and sets in the west.	3. Orion circles parallel to my horizon.
4. The Southern Cross rises in the SE and sets in the SW.	4. The Southern Cross almost rises at my S horizon.	4. The Southern Cross remains far below my horizon.
5. All of the stars rise above my horizon.	5. Most of the stars rise above my horizon.	5. Half of the stars always stay above my horizon.
6. In June the sun culminates north of my zenith. In December it culminates south.	6. In June the sun culminates high in the south. In December it culminates low in the south.	6. In June the sun never sets. In December it never rises.

Answers

1a. The Polaris Straw now points to Polaris above my N horizon.

1b. The equinox sun rises due east, culminates to my south and sets due west.

2a. The Polaris Straw now points to Polaris on the equator-person's N horizon.

2b. The equinox sun rises due east, culminates at the equator-person's zenith, and sets due west.

3a. The Polaris Straw now points to Polaris at the north-pole-person's zenith.

3b. The equinox sun moves full circle around the north pole person's horizon.

5b. At your home latitude, these constellations move <u>at an angle</u> to your horizon.

6. At the equator, these constellations move <u>perpendicular</u> to your horizon.

7. At the north pole these constellations move <u>parallel</u> to your horizon.

8. Students should count the total number of concepts they understand and write that number.

✓ <u>Star Jar</u> (with water horizon): Is the jar half filled with water up to the Celestial Equator? Does it leak when you shake it? Is the Southern Cross fixed to the lid a little behind Leo?

Materials

☐ The Pointer Box and Sun Protractor.
☐ The Star Jar with attached clay "sun."
☐ A source of water.
☐ A small bottle of food coloring with dropper dispenser. Blue is the most realistic color. If you don't want your students to handle concentrated food coloring, mix a quart jar of colored water in advance.
☐ Plastic wrap.
☐ The Round Map cutout.
☐ Scissors.
☐ Clear tape or glue.

DIPPER BOX

1. Seal an empty cereal box shut with masking tape, and lay it on its side. Run more tape along the *top* edge so half of its sticky side remains free.

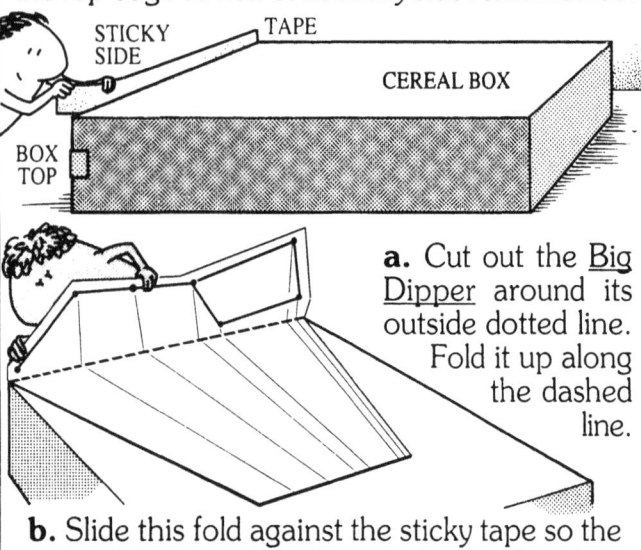

a. Cut out the Big Dipper around its outside dotted line. Fold it up along the dashed line.

b. Slide this fold against the sticky tape so the Big Dipper stands up, centered along the edge.

2. Cut out the View Point around its dotted line.

a. Fold both wings underneath to make a stiff triangular shape. Fold down the end circle on the dashed line.

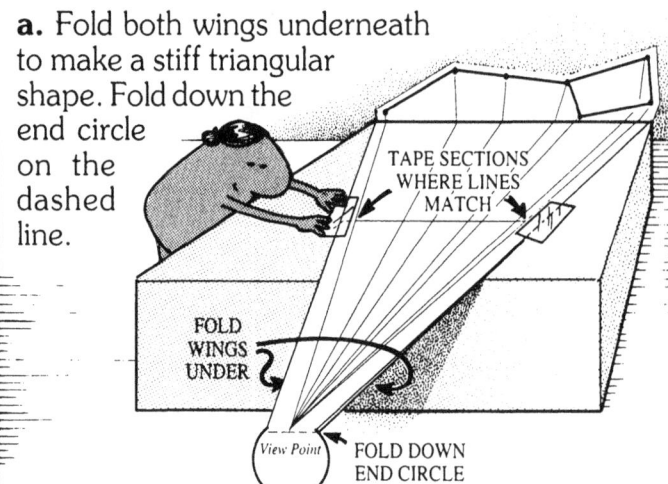

b. Match the lines on both papers so they run straight from the view point to the Dipper pattern. Stick both pieces to the box with clear tape where they meet.

3. Stick 7 pins (not 6) into the box at the center of each tiny circle. Use a penny to pad your finger.

a. Hold the view point circle steady under one eye, with your other eye shut. Raise, lower or lean all 7 pins so each pinhead "star" matches the Big Dipper "star" behind it. Use a longer pin to reach Dubhe at the top of the Dipper cup, or tape two pins together.

b. Ancient Arab astronomers saw this same pattern of Big Dipper stars in the night sky that *we see* today. List the names they gave to each star.

c. You and the sun occupy the same point in this model. Where is the sun (our nearest star) in this model?

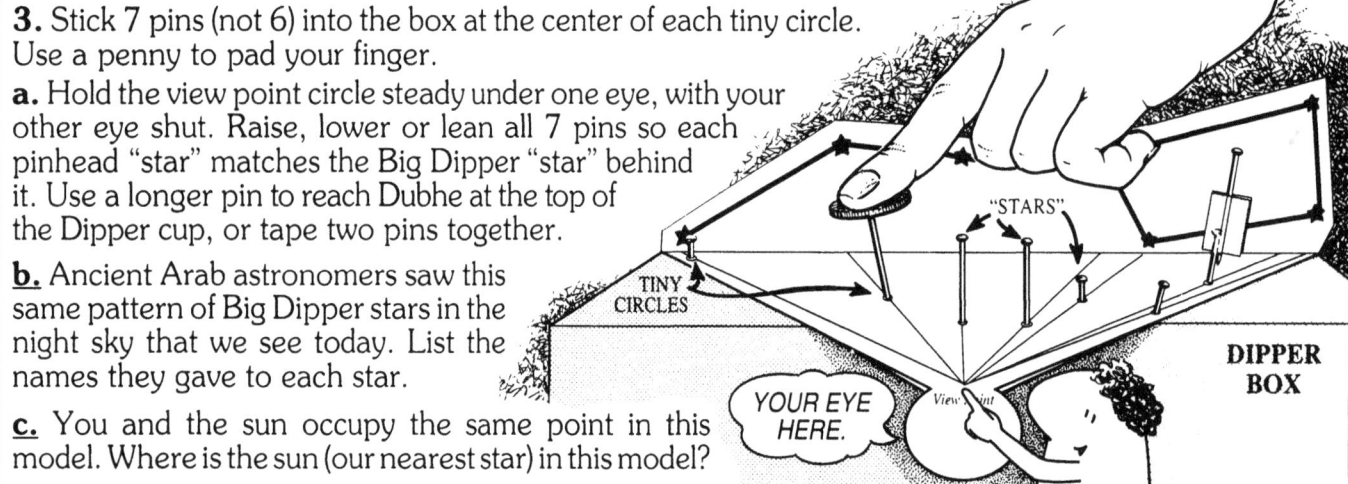

4. When viewed from the sun (our home star), these 7 pinhead "stars" seem to form a "dipper" shape.

a. Do you see this same shape when viewing these pinhead "stars" from other directions? Explain.

b. On the Dipper pattern, Alkaid and Mizar appear to be a closer star pair than Mizar and Dubhe. Is this actually the case? Explain.

c. Which star is *actually* closer to Mizar, Alkaid or our own Sun?

5. View the pinhead "stars" from Alkaid against a paper background on your desk. Balance the box on one corner with the view point gently curved (not folded) underneath.

a. Draw dots to mark the apparent positions of the 6 stars.

b. Connect your dots. Label each star, then name this alien constellation.

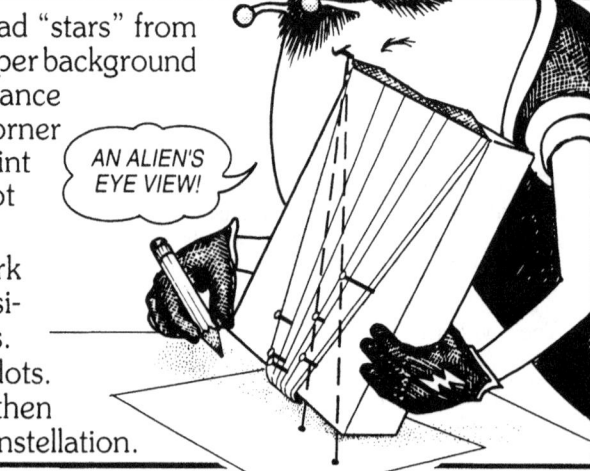

Objective

To distinguish between the actual positions of stars in space and their apparent positions on the celestial sphere.

Supporting Concepts

Hold your thumb in front of the teacher's head so both objects have the same *apparent size*. Do these objects have the same *actual size*? Discuss the difference.

Lesson Notes

2a, 2b. These folded wings reinforce the overhanging platform, and provide a slight lift to compensate for natural sagging. If this upward slope is too exaggerated, try applying extra tape nearer to the edge of the box.

3a. This operation requires concentrated effort to create an accurate alignment. It is easiest to do without eye glasses. Keep the view point circle gently pressed to the eye, just under the lower eyelid, while adjusting each pinhead to match its background star. Start by lining up the center pins. Then hold this alignment while adjusting the outside pins.

Answers

3b. From left to right, the Arabs named these Big Dipper stars: Alkaid, Mizar, Alioth, Megrez, Phecda, Dubhe and Merak.

3c. Our sun is located at the view point where all of the sight lines come together.

4a. No. The pinheads form a recognizable Dipper only when viewed at or very near the view point.

4b. No. Even though Alkaid and Mizar look closer on the Dipper pattern, the pinheads that model their actual location in space are much farther apart than the pinheads corresponding to Dubhe and Mizar.

4c. Our sun is the closer star! The distance between the sun's position at the view point and Mizar's pinhead is significantly less than the distance from Mizar's pinhead to Alkaid's.

5. From some hypothetical planet orbiting Alkaid, the Big Dipper looks rather like a bent spoon. Your students may draw somewhat different shapes depending on what angle they hold the box over the paper, and how accurately they mark the pinheads.

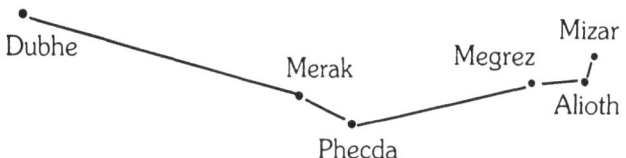

(All of the stars in the constellation Bent Spoon, with the exception of Dubhe, would appear much dimmer than they are in the Big Dipper because they are seen from a much greater distance. Stars much closer to Alkaid would likely outshine the Bent Spoon, making it very difficult to recognize. Our sun, only 1/630 as bright as Alkaid, is too dim to see in this star field except through a telescope.)

✓ Dipper Box: Is the view point platform reasonably level? Do the pins leans away from the middle? (Outer pins that stick straight up are not properly aligned.)

Extension

Q. Your Dipper model tells you which star shines most dimly. Which one is it?
A. Megrez. It is the smallest star.

Q. Cover the pinheads of Mizar and Alkaid with clay balls that are just large enough to hide these star on the Dipper pattern behind, when viewed from the sun. What can you conclude about the apparent brightness and actual brightness of these stars?

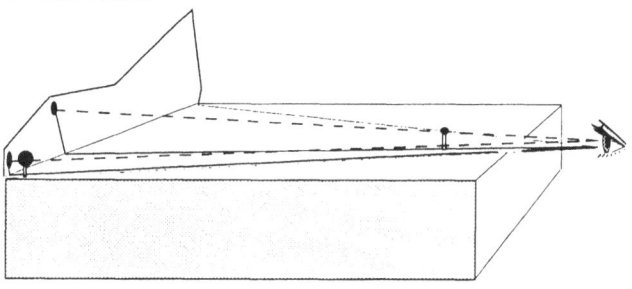

A. The Alkaid pinhead must be covered with more clay than the Mizar pinhead to hide their respective stars on the Dipper Pattern. Even though both stars *appear* to have the same size (brightness) when viewed from the sun's position, distant Alkaid is actually the bigger (brighter) star.

Materials

☐ An empty 32 ounce Grape-Nuts box. The Dipper pattern is just wide enough to fit across a box of this size from corner to corner. You may substitute larger cereal boxes, but students will need to snip the excess masking tape that remains exposed on each side of the Dipper after completing step 1, and fold it out of the way.
☐ Masking tape.
☐ Scissors.
☐ The Big Dipper cutout.
☐ The View point cutout.
☐ Clear tape.
☐ Straight pins. A standard 1 inch length is suitable. Supply a few longer pins, if available, to line up with Dubhe at the top of the Dipper cup. Otherwise students can tape two shorter pins together.
☐ A penny.

POLAR GRAPH

1. Get a Polar Graph. Find the point where 11 h (sidereal time) and 62° N (declination) intersect.

a. The star Dubhe in this Big Dipper table has these same *coordinates*. Plot the other 6 Dipper stars on your Polar Graph just like Dubhe.

b. Connect and label the dots as directed in the table.

2. Plot, connect and label stars in the other 3 tables.

THE BIG DIPPER

star name	sidereal time	declination
Dubhe	11.0 h	62° N
Merak	11.0 h	56° N
Phecda	11.9 h	54° N
Megrez	12.3 h	57° N
Alioth	12.9 h	56° N
Mizar	13.4 h	55° N
Alkaid	13.8 h	49° N

Connect stars as a cup and handle; label pattern.

CASSIOPEIA

star name	sidereal time	declination
Caph	0.2 h	59° N
Schedar	0.7 h	57° N
Navi	0.9 h	61° N
Ruchbah	1.4 h	60° N
Segin	1.9 h	64° N

Connect stars as an "M" or "W;" label pattern.

GUARDIANS OF THE POLE

star name	sidereal time	declination
Kochab	14.8 h	74° N
Pherkad	15.3 h	72° N

Connect stars with a straight line; label pattern.

POLE STAR

star name	sidereal time	declination
Polaris	2.5 h	89° N

Label it Polaris (POLE STAR).

3. Double check your work, then poke a pinhole through all 15 star positions.

4. Poke a pin through the North Celestial Pole (NCP), and aim it at Polaris. Rotate the stars around the NCP in the direction of the arrows.

a. Which *star* moves in the largest circle? Why?

b. Does the Pole Star also move in circles? Why is it considered "fixed."

c. The Big Dipper, like a signpost in the sky, always points to Polaris. Explain.

5. Stick a bit of clay on the ecliptic circle of your Star Jar at your current calendar date.

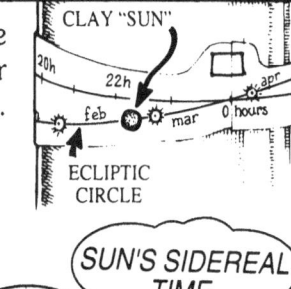

a. What is the sun's hour position on the celestial equator (its current sidereal time)?

b. Cut out the Sun Arrow. Lightly tape it to your Polar Graph with its center mark at the sun's current sidereal time.

6. Copy this table.
Use your Polar Graph to fill it in with directions like these:

Sun Arrow	12:00 NOON	6:00 PM	12:00 MIDNIGHT	6:00 AM	RIGHT NOW
THE BIG DIPPER					
CASSIOPEIA					

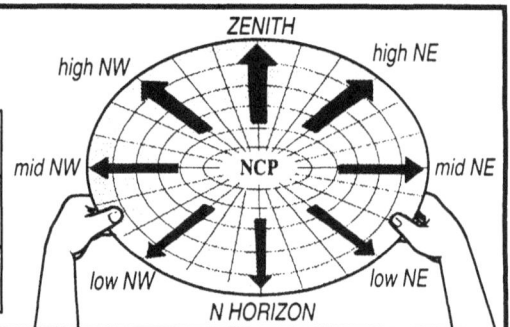

Objective

To plot star positions on a polar graph in terms of sidereal time and declination. To use the resulting star map to predict star positions in the daytime sky.

Supporting Concepts

✪ Review line values on the polar graph:
- Count sidereal times clockwise around the outside of the graph beginning with twelve hours: 12.0 hours, 12.1 hours, 12.2 hours, and so on.
- Count declinations beginning with 45° on the outer ring of the graph and continuing to 90° at the center: 45°, 46°, 47°, and so on.

Lesson Notes

1-2. Data in these tables is simplified to accommodate students with little or no previous graphing experience. Sidereal hours, normally divided into minutes and seconds, are rounded here to the nearest tenth hour. Declinations are rounded to the nearest whole degree.

3. These pinholes will be useful in step 6 of the next activity. They'll shine like tiny stars when the graph is aimed toward Polaris in the bright daytime sky.

5b. This Polar Graph is a flat projection of the shallow "bowl" shape you would get if you sliced the top off the celestial sphere around our earth. Imagine the Sun Arrow taped to its edge, pointing along the curve of this bowl to the sun behind you.

4a. Alkaid, at the end of the Dipper handle, appears to move in the largest circles around the NCP. Of all the plotted stars it is most southerly, located furthest from the NCP.

4b. Polaris moves in a very small circle around the NCP. Because this motion is too slight to notice, Polaris seems to remain fixed in the same location above your N horizon all night long, all year long.

4c. The outer edge of the Big Dipper's cup "points" to Polaris. A straight line starting at Merak and passing through Dubhe almost intersects Polaris on the graph.

5a. Students should name the sidereal hour that is closest to the clay sun they just positioned at their current calendar date on the Star Jar.

6. These north sky descriptions, ranging from your horizon to your zenith, apply reasonably well to latitudes between 30° N and 60° N. This sample table is for 9 AM in the morning of March 21st, when the sun is at a sidereal time of 0h.

Sun Arrow	12:00 NOON	6:00 PM	12:00 MIDNIGHT	6:00 AM	RIGHT NOW
The Big Dipper	N horizon	mid NE	zenith	mid NW	low NW
Cassiopeia	very high NE	above mid NW	very low NW	below mid NE	above mid NE

Answers

✓ Polar Graph:

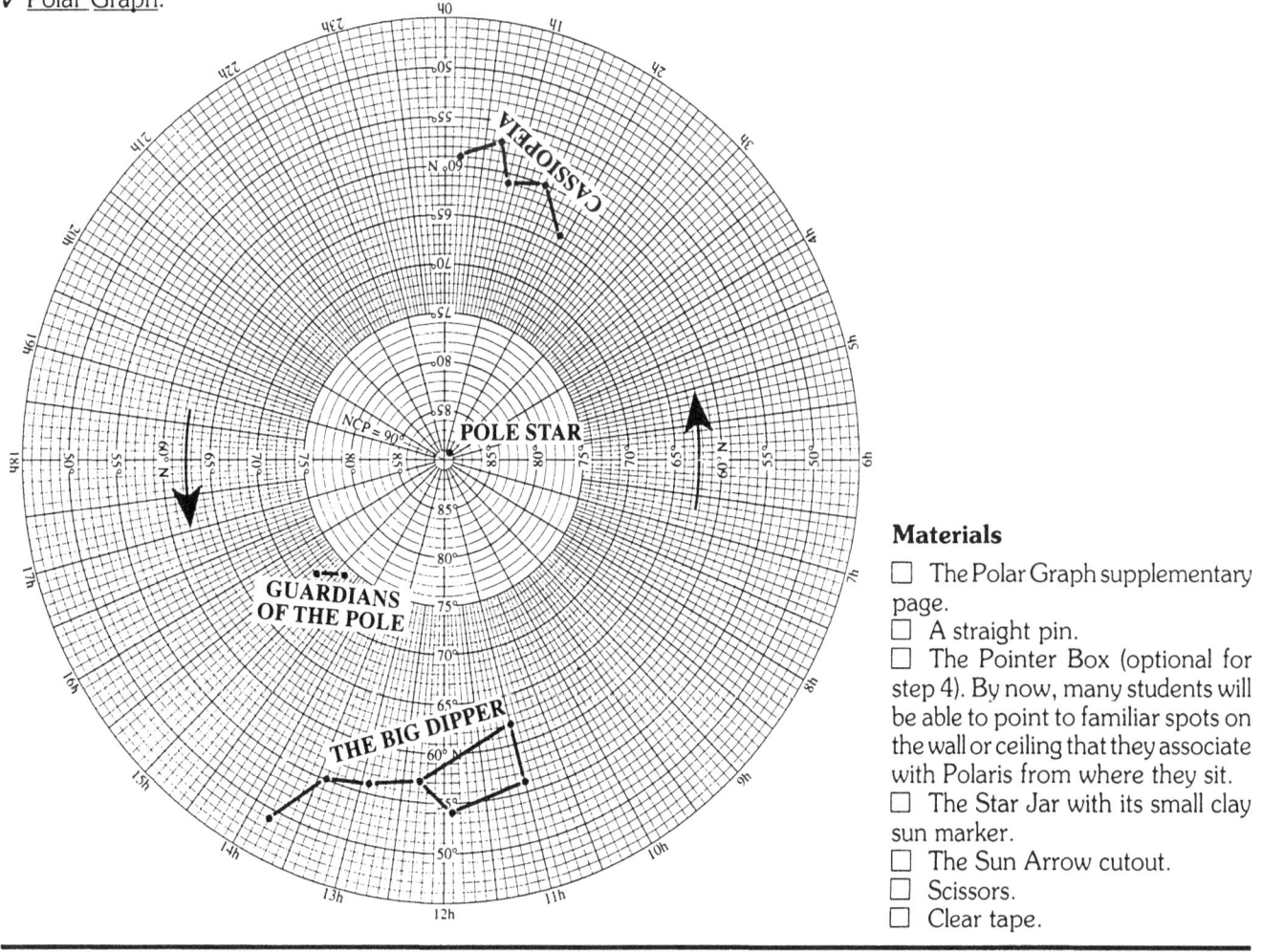

Materials

- ☐ The Polar Graph supplementary page.
- ☐ A straight pin.
- ☐ The Pointer Box (optional for step 4). By now, many students will be able to point to familiar spots on the wall or ceiling that they associate with Polaris from where they sit.
- ☐ The Star Jar with its small clay sun marker.
- ☐ The Sun Arrow cutout.
- ☐ Scissors.
- ☐ Clear tape.

THE PLANETS AND THE STARS ( )9
APPARENT SIZE

1. Carefully cut out and fold the <u>Angle Finder</u> so it looks like this:

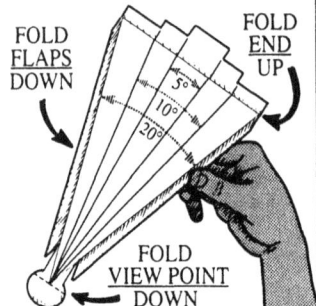

2. Tape notebook paper (holes at top) to a dark background.

a. Stand just far enough away so this paper has an *apparent* width of 5° when you touch the view point of your Angle Finder just under one eye. Mark your floor position with masking tape labeled 5°.

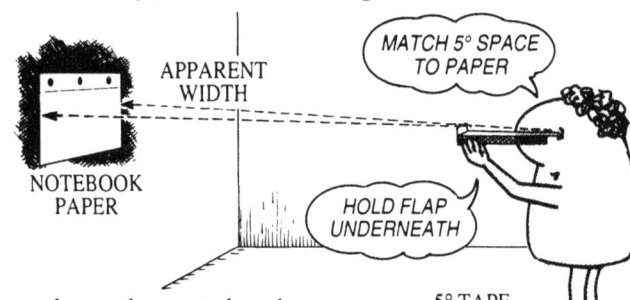

b. Mark other floor positions where the notebook paper has an apparent width of 10°; an apparent width of 20°.

c. Does the *actual* size of the paper change? Its apparent size? Explain.

3. Sight to the notebook paper from each tape marker again. This time use your Dipper Box:
a. How many degrees separate star pairs x, y and z?
b. Label the 5° star pair inside the Dipper "cup" on your Polar Graph.

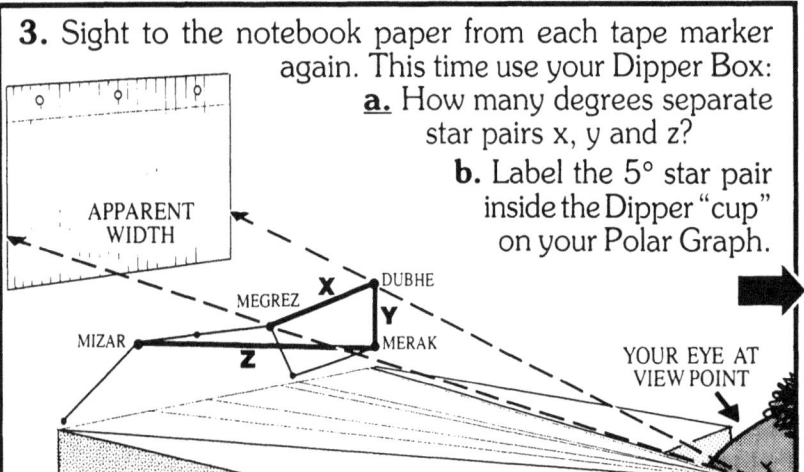

4. Fold back your Polar Graph at the 11 hour line. Extend the fold across the page.

a. Stand at the 5° marker. Hold the graph close enough to your face so the 5° separation between Merak and Dubhe matches the apparent 5° width of the paper on the wall.

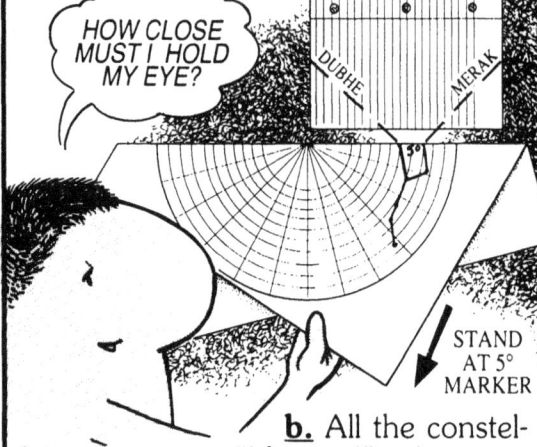

b. All the constellations appear "life-sized" when you hold the graph this close. Measure the arrow equal to this "actual size" viewing distance at the top of your Polar Graph.

5. Your *fully extended* arm and hand is an angle finder!
a. Stand at each tape marker to verify that these angles are correct.
b. Trace around your hand, fingers fully spread. Mark these angles and memorize them.
c. Imagine stretching your arm and hand toward the Big Dipper in the night sky. On your tracing, label which finger spaces span which stars.

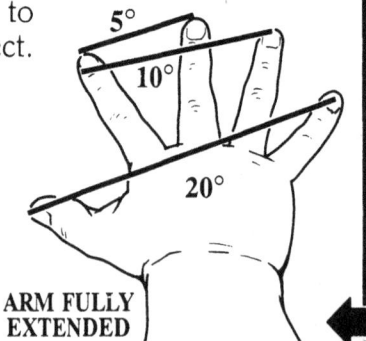

6. Hold your Polar Graph against the sky so daylight shines through all the pinholes.
a. How will you match the Polaris pinhole to Polaris in the sky?
b. Where will you point the Sun Arrow so all the "stars" circle to their current positions?
c. How far will you hold it from your face so every pinhole on the graph matches its star behind?

7. Show a family member these same stars at home, on a clear dark night.
a. Take a flashlight with you. Rubberband red cellophane or tissue over the light so you can read the Polar Graph without losing your night vision.
b. Answer the questions under your Polar Graph as weather permits.

Copyright © 1994 by TOPS Learning Systems, Canby OR 97013. Reproduction limited to personal classroom use.

Objective

To estimate the apparent separation between stars in the Big Dipper. To observe polar constellations in the night sky.

Supporting Concepts

◉ As a class exercise, ask everyone to hold their outstretched arms at these angles. Ask volunteers to name classroom objects with these apparent separations.

◉ Two fingers held at arm's length measure an *apparent separation* of about 5°. (See box 5 on the left.)
• Ask volunteers to name classroom objects with this apparent separation.
• Draw two "stars" on your blackboard about 1 hand span apart. Ask if these are separated by more or less than 5°. Encourage students in the front of the room to argue with students in the back. (Angles of separation depend on the location of the observer. That is why they are called "apparent" separations.)
• Can observers agree about the apparent separation between two real stars in the night sky? (Yes. Real stars are so far away from our pinpoint earth, everyone essentially stands at the same point in space.)

Lesson Notes

1. This Angle Finder looks similar to, but should not be confused with, the View Point cutout that is now a part of the Dipper Box.

2-3. Both the Angle Finder in step 2 and the Dipper Box in step 3 are used the same way: hold each view point under one eye, close the other eye, then site to each side of the notebook paper.

5a. Both children and adults should find these angles quite accurate. Short fingers on short arms span about the same number of degrees as long fingers on long arms because hands and arms grow proportionally.

6. This exercise can be done indoor or outdoors. The advantage of going outside is to allow bright sky light to illuminate the star holes from behind, adding a touch of realism. Staying inside, of course, increases your class control. If you have north-facing windows, combine the best of both options. In any case, students should think before they act, answering questions a, b and c before "observing" the daytime stars.

Answers

2c. The notebook paper on the wall does not change its actual size. It appears larger only because you stand closer to it; it appears smaller because you stand farther away.

3a. x. Megrez to Dubhe = 10° separation
y. Dubhe to Merak = 5° separation
z. Merak to Mizar = 20° separation

4b. The arrow labeled "Viewing Distance for Actual Size" measures 16 cm.

5b-5c.

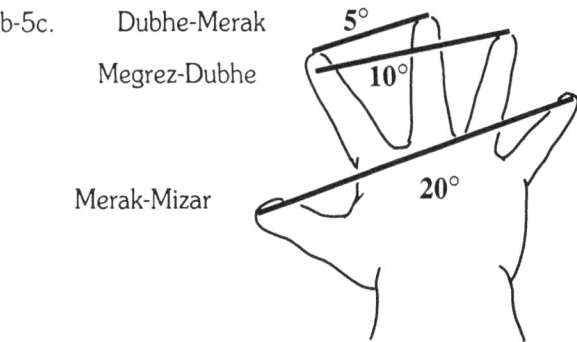

6a. Align your Pointer Box to its outside landmark. Aim the Polaris pinhole (or more accurately, the NCP) in the same direction as the Polaris Straw points.

6b. Keeping the graph pointed at Polaris, rotate it until the Sun Arrow matches the position of the sun behind you.

6c. Spread your fingers just wide enough to match the 16 cm viewing-distance arrow. Using your hand as a spacer, hold your graph this distance from your face. All the tiny pinhole stars you now see match what you would see in the sky right now if the stars were not obscured by sunlight or clouds.

✓ Polar Graph: Does it have a crease indicating that it was folded back along the 11 hour line? Is the 5° separation between Dubhe and Merak labeled *inside* the Dipper cup? Are all the data boxes completed (weather permitting)? Has the apparent separation between Dubhe and Polaris been determined? (It is about 28°). Is Alcor correctly drawn and labeled?

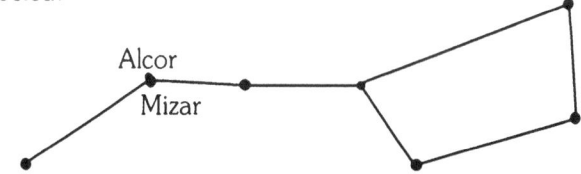

(Alcor and Mizar are an optical double. They are relatively close in astronomical terms, about 1 LY apart, but do not orbit each other as a binary system. They do, however, share a common history. Alcor and Mizar were compressed by gravity from a common nebula of gas and dust, along with Alioth, Megrez, Phecda, Merak, and many other stars. Together they drift through space as members of the same star cluster. We don't see these stars as a cluster because we are inside it, though our sun is not a member.)

Materials

☐ The Angle Finder cutout.
☐ Scissors.
☐ A sheet of notebook paper.
☐ Masking tape.
☐ The Dipper Box.
☐ The Polar Graph.
☐ The Pointer Box. Students may or many not need this to estimate the position of Polaris in the daytime sky.
☐ A flashlight with red cellophane, tissue paper or piece of a red plastic bag rubberbanded over the light. Students will use this equipment at home.

THE PLANETS AND THE STARS ( )10

LOTS-O-DOTS

1. Tape a magnifying glass to the bottom of a small jar so it overhangs as far as possible.

a. Get 10 sheets of <u>Lots-o-Dots</u>. Cut out just *one* tiny dot from one of the sheets. (Leave yourself a paper "handle" so you can easily hold the dot.)

b. Tape this dot to clean notebook paper. Label it "**1 dot**."

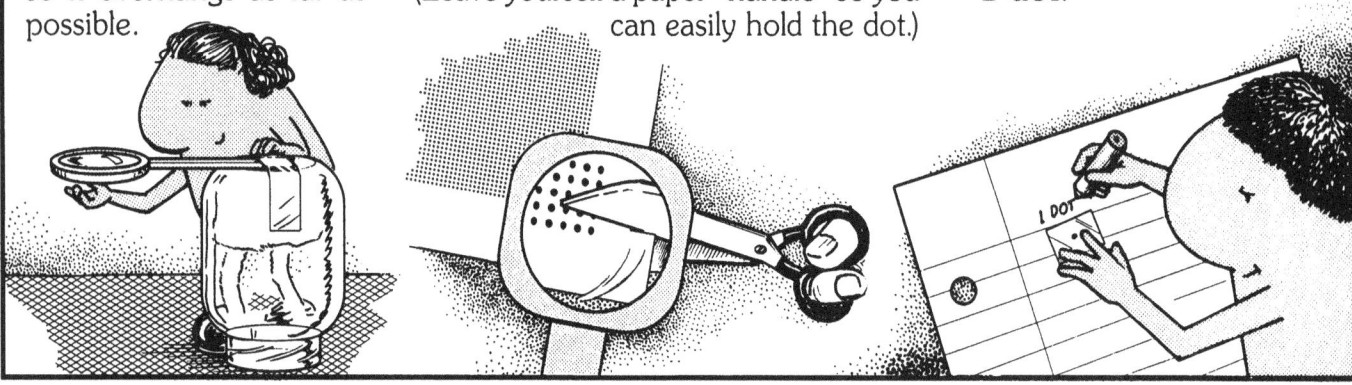

2. Cut and tape these groups of dots to your paper. Show math next to each group that tells how you decided on its size and shape.

- 10 dots
- 100 dots
- 1,000 dots
- 10,000 dots

3. Cover the *back* of your notebook paper with **100,000 dots**. Show your math.

HOW MUCH LESS THAN ONE SHEET?

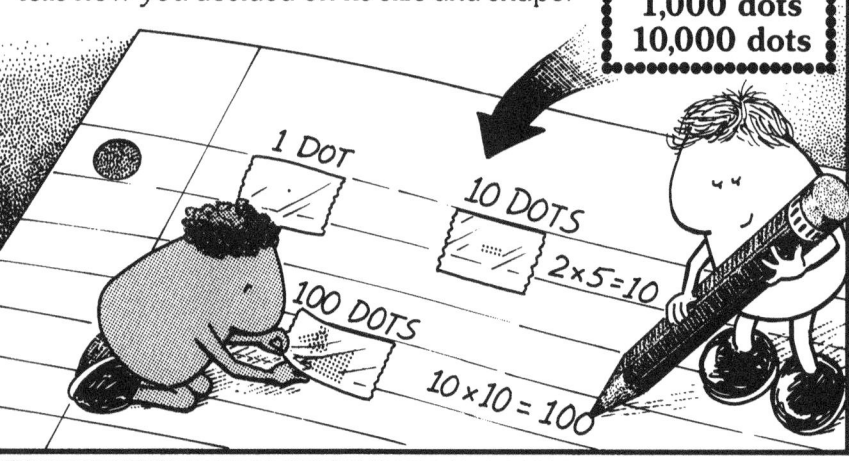

4. How many *whole* Lots-o-Dots sheets (plus a *part* of one more) total **1,000,000 dots** (one million). Show your math on the bottom front of your notebook paper.

IF EACH SHEET HAS...

5. Cover a full sheet of newspaper with one million dots!

a. Trim each Lots-o-Dots sheet to the outside line. Overlap the grid numbers so they show only once between large blocks of dots.

b. You'll need to divide some sheets so they all fit inside the newspaper borders. Tape down all pieces at the corners. Use tape sparingly.

c. Label it "**One Million Dots**."

CUT APART DOT SHEETS TO MAKE THEM FIT.

FULL SHEET (2 PAGES) NEWSPAPER

Copyright © 1994 by TOPS Learning Systems, Canby OR 97013. Reproduction limited to personal classroom use.

Objective

To develop a concrete understanding of the quantity *one million*. To appreciate the dramatic increases that result from an exponential expansion.

Supporting Concepts

◯ Draw a 4 by 5 array of circles on your blackboard. Must you count all the circles to know their total number? (No. Simply count the number of circles along adjacent sides, then multiply both totals together: 5 x 4 = 20.)

◯ Hold up a sheet of Lots-o-Dots. How many dots are in this 300 by 400 dot grid?

$$300 \times 400 = 120,000$$

◯ An easy way to multiply large numbers is to drop the place-holding zeros, and add them to your answer:

Examples:
<u>3</u>00 x <u>4</u>00 = <u>3 x 4</u> + four zeros = <u>12</u>0,000
<u>5</u>0 x <u>2</u>00 = <u>5 x 2</u> + three zeros = <u>10</u>,000
<u>1</u>,000 x <u>1</u>,000 = <u>1 x 1</u> + six zeros = <u>1</u>,000,000

◯ On your blackboard write a one followed by 9 zeros:

1 0 0 0 0 0 0 0 0 0

Using a pencil as a pointer, name each decimal place from one to a billion:
(one, ten, hundred, thousand, ten thousand, hundred thousand, million, ten million, hundred million, billion.)

Lesson Notes

This TOPS module is based on an American system of numeration. Beyond 1 million, the British system is somewhat different:

<u>American System</u>
one, thousand, million, billion, trillion, quadrillion

<u>British System</u>
one, thousand, million, milliard, billion, trillion

To adapt this book to the British system, first change every *billion* you see to "milliard." Then change every *trillion* you see to "billion."

1. Because the magnifiers are novel, most everyone will enjoy using them. But younger students, in particular, may soon abandon their hand lenses for these reasons:
• Young eyes accommodate to very close working distances. They can enlarge these dots simply by looking close.
• The magnifier's small size requires too much eye-hand coordination to keep scissors and dots within its small field of view.
• The magnifier is properly used with both eyes open. Younger children in particular tend to close one eye, which, over time, can cause eye strain.

1a. A corner dot is easiest to isolate, using the corner itself as a handle.

2-3. Encourage students to leave the grid numbers attached. This makes the dots easy to count.

Answers

1b. Students should tape a single dot near the top of their assignment sheet and label it "1 dot."

2. Students should tape these dot arrays (or others that equal the same numbers) to their assignment sheet:
2 x 5 array = 10 dots
10 x 10 array = 100 dots
10 x 100 array = 1,000 dots
100 x 100 array = 10,000 dots

3. One way to get 100,000 dots is to cut off a 400 x 50 array (20,000 dots) from the side of a full sheet of 120,000 dots.

4. Eight sheets of 120,000 dots equals 960,000 dots. Add a 400 x 100 array (40,000 dots) to total 1,000,000 dots.

✓ <u>Million Dot Sheet</u>: Is the newspaper covered by 8 1/4 Lots-o-Dot sheets? Is it labeled "One Million Dots?"

Extension

Q. Ask one or two of your students to set up a bulletin board display with 2 newspapers covered with a million dots each, and a pin, thread and tape.

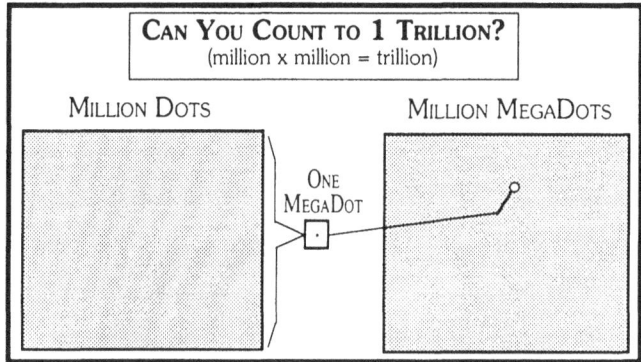

A. This display can lead to a mind-stretching discussion: To count <u>each</u> megadot you have to first count the million dots it represents. Counting nonstop at 1 dot per second, this would take:

1,000,000 sec x 1 hr/3600 sec x 1 day/24 hrs = 11.6 days

To count each megadot, it would take:

11.6 million days x 1 yr/365 days = 31,700 years

If you somehow managed to do this job for a generation of 31.7 years (perhaps counting 2 dots a second and taking time off), and then handed the job down to your son or daughter for another 31.7 years, and so on, your 1,000th generation ancestor down the line would finish the job!

Materials

☐ A hand lens.
☐ Masking tape.
☐ A baby food jar.
☐ Ten sheets of Lots-o-Dots per student or activity group. Photocopy these, as usual, from the dot master at the back of this book. Use the blank side of old photocopies to conserve paper.
☐ Blunt children's scissors. Long, pointed scissors are a special hazard to younger, uncoordinated children because of the close nature of the paper cutting work.
☐ Notebook paper.
☐ Clear tape.
☐ A full sheet (2 leaves or 4 pages) of a standard-sized newspaper. Tabloids are too small.

LIGHT LIGHTNING

1. Get a <u>Kilometer</u> Bar.
a. Write the value of each decimal place in the *top* pointer spaces, from **one k** to **1 trillion k**.

USE WORDS, NOT NUMBERS.

b. Beyond one trillion k, record place values as *powers of ten*, out to 10^{24} **k**.
<u>**c.**</u> How many zeros are in the number 10^{24}?

2. One kilometer equals 0.62 miles, about 2.5 laps around a quarter-mile track.

a. Find the equation *1 kilometer = 2.5 laps* in the bottom pointer space under the *ones* decimal place. Write similar equations for 10 k, 100 k and 1,000 k in the next 3 pointer spaces.
b. Extend the equation in the first pointer space to *1 kilometer = 2.5 laps = 0.62 miles*. Extend the next 3 equations in the same manner.
<u>**c.**</u> What happens to the distance on the bar each time you move the decimal one zero to the right?

3. Light travels about 300 thousand kilometers in 1 second, almost far enough to reach the moon!
a. Record this distance for *one light second* in its pointer space. Use zeros.

EARTH TO MOON
ONE LIGHT SECOND

1 LIGHT SECOND

<u>**b.**</u> Outline this number of dots with a yellow marker on your Million Dot newspaper sheet. Show your math.

4. The earth and sun are 150 million kilometers apart. This is called *one astronomical unit* (1 AU).

EARTH TO SUN
ONE ASTRONOMICAL UNIT (1 AU)

a. Record this distance in its pointer space. Use zeros.
<u>**b.**</u> Assemble 48 full-sized sheets of newsprint into your own special edition of a newspaper. Add your Million Dot Sheet (1 layer newsprint + 1 layer Lots-o-Dots) as the front page. If these 50 layers were printed with a million dots each, how many total dots would you have?
<u>**c.**</u> Think of each dot as a "travel token" good for one kilometer. Headline this special edition with the number of "tokens" inside. Is this enough to reach the sun?

5. Light travels about 1 billion kilometers in 1 hour! This is almost far enough to reach the planet Saturn when it is closest to Earth.
a. Record this distance for *one light hour* in its part of the pointer space. Use words.
<u>**b.**</u> Pile together your special headline edition with those of your classmates until you get a Billion Token STACK. How many special editions are needed for a one-way trip to Saturn?

SATURN TO EARTH
ONE LIGHT HOUR

Objective

To develop an understanding of astronomical distances within our solar system. To define the speed of light.

Lesson Notes

5b. If your students are self-paced, 20 newspaper editions will take a while to accumulate. That's OK. Pick a convenient location in your classroom (in a corner perhaps, or against a wall) to place the first newspaper edition that comes in. Stick a horizontal strip of masking tape 52 cm above the floor to represent the height that this STACK will eventually reach. Label it like this:

One Billion Kilometer Tokens Reach This High!

This visual aid is now available for immediate reference in the next activity.

Answers

1c. The number 10^{24} has 24 zeros.

2c. Each time you move the decimal point 1 place to the right, you increase the bar distance 10 times.

3b. A full 300 by 400 Lots-o-Dots sheet contains 120,000 dots. Two sheets contain 240,000 dots. Another half sheet of 60,000 dots totals 300,000 dots. Students should thus outline a total of 2 1/2 Lots-o-Dots sheets.

4b. 50 layers x 1 million dots/layer = 50 million dots

4c. Students should write a bold headline across their 50 layer (200 page) newspaper edition that conveys how many travel tokens are inside:

DOTS DOTS DOTS: 50 million kilometer tokens inside!

This many tokens reach only a third of the way to the sun. (This is not a place you'd really want to see up close anyway.)

5b. Twenty Special Edition newspapers add up to a billion dot STACK, enough for a one-way trip to Saturn:

20 editions x 50 million tokens/edition =
= 1,000 million tokens
= 1 billion tokens.

(Or think of this as 1,000 layers of a million tokens each.)

✓ Kilometer Bar: Student responses are shown below in bold type. Empty pointer spaces will be completed in activities that follow.

✓ Million Dot Newspaper: Are 2 1/2 sheets of Lots-o-Dots outlined with a marking pen?

Extension

Q. The first 4 major divisions on the Kilometer Bar are 1, 10, 100, and 1,000. Write out a longer sequence of numbers that count all the divisions in between as well. Begin at 1 k and end at 1 light second:

1 k, 2 k, 3 k, 4 k, ..., 9 k, 10 k, 20 k, 30 k, ...,
..., 100,000 k, 200,000 k, 300,000 k = 1 LS.

Materials

☐ The Kilometer Bar sheet.
☐ The Million Dot Newspaper sheet from activity 10.
☐ A yellow crayon or marker to outline dots; a dark marker to headline the 50 layer (200 page) newspaper edition.
☐ Fifty standard-sized sheets of newsprint per student. Multiplying this requirement by at least 20 students translates into a 2 foot stack of newsprint, minimum, plus perhaps an additional foot to compensate for half-sized sheets and magazine supplements. To avoid hauling this yard of newsprint into your classroom by yourself, assign step 4b and 4c as homework.

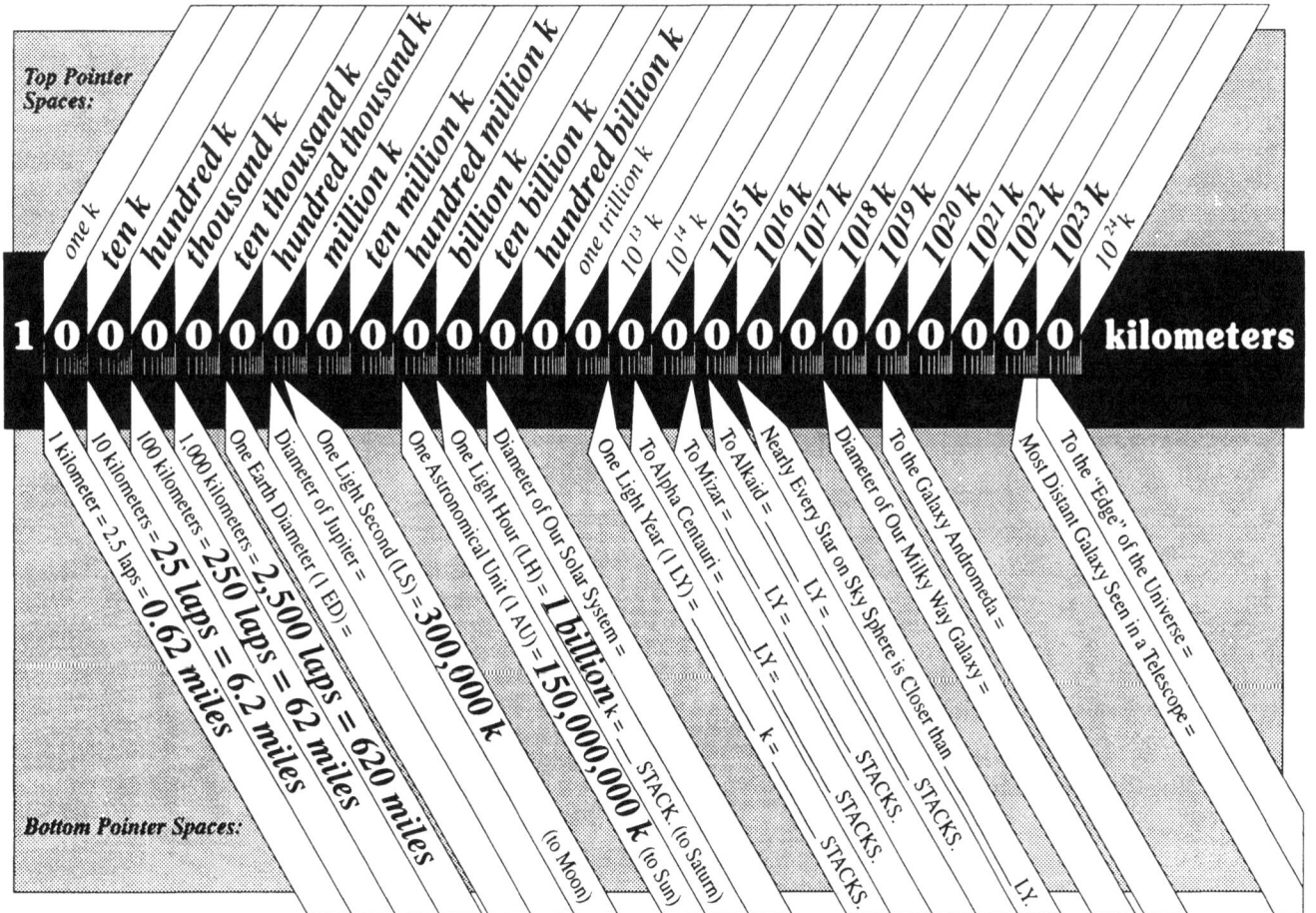

THE PLANETS AND THE STARS (   )12

STAR TRAVEL

1. You can travel 1 billion kilometers with the STACK of kilometer tokens on your classroom floor. Write "1" on the line inside the 1 Light Hour pointer space of your Kilometer Bar.

a. Light travels 10 trillion kilometers in 1 Light Year. Write this distance (in words) in its pointer space.
b. How many zeros on the bar do you pass jumping from 1 LH to 1 LY? How many STACKS of kilometer tokens take you 1 LY? Write your answer on the correct line.

2. Alpha Centauri (the nearest star to our sun) is 4.3 light years away. On your Kilometer Bar, record this distance in LY; in STACKS of kilometer tokens.

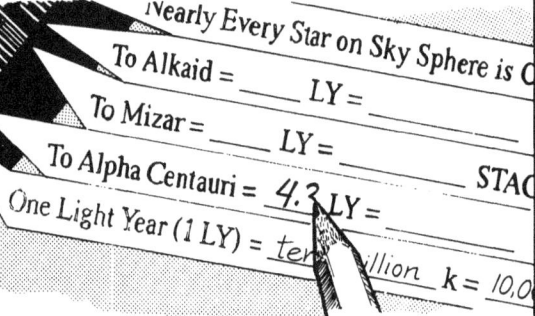

a. Use information on your Dipper Box to complete both parts of the pointer spaces for Mizar and Alkaid.
b. The starlight we see at night is "old" light. Explain, using an example.

3. Cut around the dotted line of the <u>Star Ruler</u>. Fold it lengthwise along the 3 solid lines. Tape the long edges together while it's flat, then open it into a box.

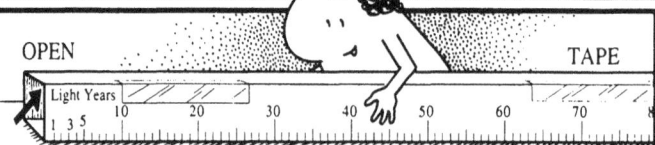

4. The <u>light years</u> side of this ruler measures the *actual* distance between stars on your Dipper Box.

a. Does this Star Ruler measure LY distances similar to those written on your Dipper Box? Explain.

b. Use your Star Ruler to show that Alkaid is farther away from every other Dipper star than *you* are! Explain how you did this.

5. The <u>degrees</u> side of this ruler measures the *apparent* separation between stars on the cup and handle of your Dipper Box.

a. Confirm that the 3 apparent star separations you found before are about right.
b. Which stars have the widest apparent separation? What is it? How should you hold both hands to span this angle when you observe the Big Dipper at night?

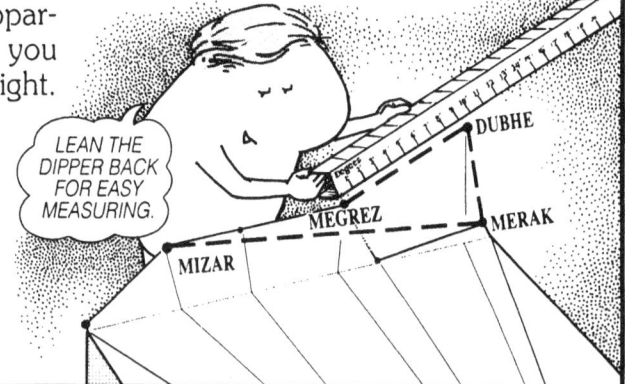

6. In the neighborhood of the Big Dipper, stars are scattered with the <u>average spacing</u> shown on your ruler of 1 star per cube. Most of these stars are too dim to see with the naked eye.

a. Which 2 Dipper stars are actually separated by this average space? How many LY's is this?

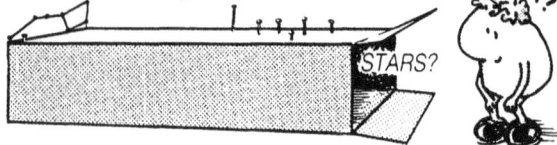

b. The cereal box models a small part our star neighborhood. How many stars would you expect to find inside this volume of space?

Copyright © 1994 by TOPS Learning Systems, Canby OR 97013. Reproduction limited to personal classroom use.

Objective

To distinguish between *actual* star distances, measured in LY, and *apparent* star separations, measured in degrees. To appreciate the vast magnitude of interstellar space.

Lesson Notes

1b. Each jump up the Kilometer Bar is another multiple of ten. Starting with 1 LH = 1 STACK, up we climb 4 zeros:
10 LH = 10 STACKS
100 LH = 100 STACKS
1,000 LH = 1,000 STACKS
10,000 LH = 1 LY = 10,000 STACKS

Answers

1b. There are 4 zeros between 1 LS and 1 LH.

2b. Starlight travels across vast distances to reach us on Earth. The light we now see shining from Mizar, for example, left that star 88 years earlier. (Students might subtract 88 years off their current calendar year to calculate the date when this light originally left Mizar.)

4a. Yes. Using the ruler to measure from our sun at the view point to the various Dipper stars gives LY distances that are nearly the same as those listed on the Dipper Box. (Small differences are due to measuring error and each pinhead's approximate placement in space.)

4b. From Alkaid to Dubhe measures about 122 LY on the Star Ruler. This is greater than the 105 LY distance from Dubhe to our sun. The rest of the Dipper stars are closer still.

5a. Measuring apparent separations with the Star Ruler yields these approximate results:
Megrez to Dubhe = 9.7° ≈ 10°
Dubhe to Merak = 4.8° ≈ 5°
Merak to Mizar = 19.1° ≈ 20°
These measurements all fall within 1° of previous hand estimates.

5b. Alkaid and Dubhe have the widest apparent separation, almost 25°. (This is slightly more than the separation between Alkaid and Merak.)

To estimate this separation with your hands, stretch them at full arm's length in front of you. Fully spread the fingers on one hand to estimate 20°. Hold up 2 fingers on the other hand in a "victory sign" to estimate 5°. Bring your hands together so fingers touch, spanning 25°.

6a. Alioth and Megrez are separated by this average spacing. It is a little more than 7 LY.

6b. Answers will vary, depending on the volume of the cereal box. Here are the measurements for a 32 ounce Grape Nuts box:
length holds 19 stars
width holds 13.5 stars
height holds 4 stars
Estimated stars in box = 19 x 13.5 x 4 = 1026 stars

✓ Kilometer Bar: Current entries are in **bold** type.
To Alkaid = **210** LY = **2,100,000** STACKS.
To Mizar = **88** LY = **880,000** STACKS.
To Alpha Centauri = **4.3** LY = **43,000** STACKS.
One Light Year (LY) = **10 trillion** k = **10,000** STACKS.
(empty pointer space)
One Light Hour (LH) = 1 billion k = **1** STACK. (to Saturn)

Extension

Q. A STACK of Lots-o-Dots containing 1 billion kilometer tokens is about 1/2 meter high. If you stacked together enough tokens to reach Alpha Centauri, the star nearest our sun, how high would this pile reach?

A. According to the Kilometer Bar,
to Alpha Centauri = 4.3 LY = 43,000 STACKS
43,000 STACKS x 0.5 m/STACK = 21,500 m
21,500 m = 21.5 kilometers = 13.4 miles
(Just one newspaper layer from this pile takes you a million kilometers, almost 25 times around the earth!)

Q. Deep space probes L and R are located on opposite sides of the sun, about 8 LY away, at the ends of the view point's fold line. A camera on each probe beams back a picture of the Big Dipper from these deep space positions. Draw the Dipper image that each camera sees. (Hint: use thread to estimate star shifts.)

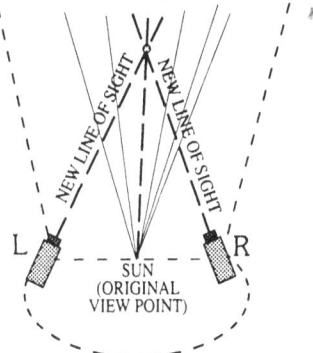

A. Moving the eye left or right causes the pinhead stars to apparently shift in the opposite direction. Closer stars, like Megrez, shift the most. Distant stars, like Alkaid, shift the least. This effect is called parallax.

To estimate the parallax shift of each star, students should stretch thread from each space probe position, across each pinhead star to its new apparent position on the celestial sphere. They will draw new Dipper shapes that look like these.

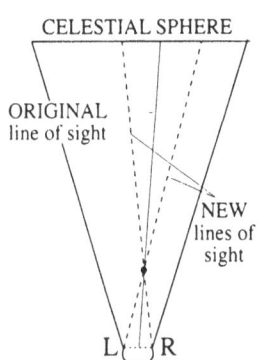

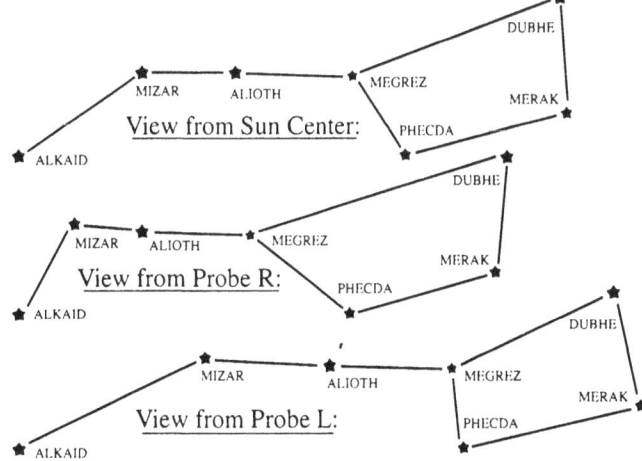

View from Sun Center:

View from Probe R:

View from Probe L:

Materials

☐ The Kilometer Bar.
☐ The STACK of 1 billion kilometer tokens, or a representation of its eventual 52 cm height.
☐ The Dipper Box.
☐ The Star Ruler cutout.
☐ Scissors and clear tape.

THE PLANETS AND THE STARS ( )13

OUR SOLAR SYSTEM

1. Carefully cut the Sun Ruler along the dashed lines into 2 strips.

a. Join the strips at the 20 AU mark with clear tape to make one long ruler. Use your table edge to keep it straight.

b. Stick a square of masking tape to the *back* of the 0 AU mark. Poke a pinhole through the dot.

2. Tape 2 sheets of notebook paper together end to end, holes down.

a. Fold them in half lengthwise to make a long crease line, then open it back up. Fold *only* the left sheet in half to make a second crease that crosses the first.

b. Stick a square of masking tape to the back where these folds cross. Poke a pinhole at this intersection.

3. Stick a pin *up* through the hole in the notebook paper, then up through the hole in the Sun Ruler. Anchor it with a lump of clay.

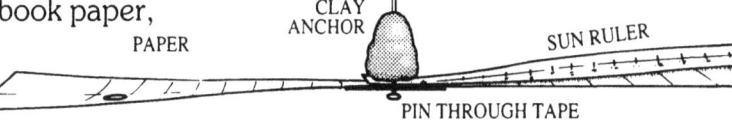

a. Cut around the *outside* dashed lines of the Solar System Squares. (Don't cut them apart.)

b. Poke a pinhole in the ruler at Pluto's orbit distance around the sun. Notice this is given in Astronomical Units (AU), not in Earth Diameters (ED).

c. Drill a sharp pencil point into the hole just far enough to draw the curve of Pluto's orbit across your paper. Label it "Pluto's Orbit."

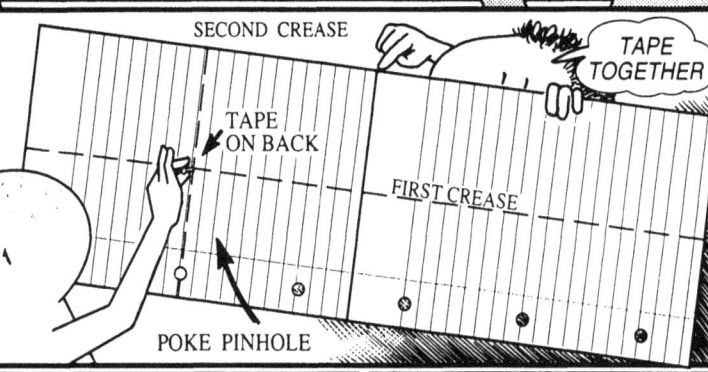

d. Draw and label the orbits of the other planets as well, working inward. (Cut off excess ruler as it gets in your way. To draw the smallest orbits, remove the clay anchor.)

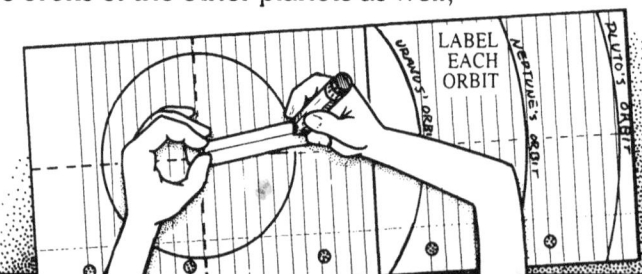

4. Remove the pin and clay. You have just drawn a scale model of our solar system with a pinhole "sun" at the center.

a. The diameter of the sun at this scale is less than 0.1 mm. Measure this pinhole "sun" with the small ruler on the side of the Sun Square. Is it the correct size?

b. Light takes about 8 minutes to travel from the sun to the earth. How long does sunlight take to reach Mars? To reach Jupiter?

c. What is the diameter of our solar system (in AU) from one side of Pluto's orbit to the other? Mark this distance on your Kilometer Bar.

Copyright © 1994 by TOPS Learning Systems, Canby OR 97013. Reproduction limited to personal classroom use.

Objective

To draw the paths of the orbiting planets in our solar system to scale.

Lesson Notes

1. This operation is easier with one person holding each half of the ruler along the table edge, while another applies the tape. Those working alone might temporarily stick one of the ruler sections to the table with masking tape.

3d. The orbits become more difficult to draw as they decrease in size. Less coordinated students may need to hold the paper as well as their pencil and the pin. Again, those working alone can temporarily stick paper to the table with masking tape.

4. Though this scale model is *close* to a true representation of the planetary orbits, it is not exact. Each planet actually orbits the sun in a slight *ellipse*, with the sun at one of its 2 focus points. (See Extension.)

Answers

4a The pinhole is too big to represent the sun. It measures about 1 mm across. (A tiny pin prick would be more to scale.)

4b. Light travels at a constant speed out from the sun. It takes proportionally longer to reach Mars and Jupiter because these planets are farther away:
time to Mars = 8 min x 1.5 AU/1.0 AU = 12 minutes
time to Jupiter = 8 min x 11.2 AU/1.0 AU ≈ 90 minutes

4c. If the radius of the solar system is taken as Pluto's average orbiting distance, then its diameter is twice that:
2 x 39 AU = 78 AU.

✓ Scale Drawing of Planetary Orbits: Are Mercury, Venus, Earth and Mars drawn relatively close to the sun? Are Jupiter, Saturn, Uranus, Neptune and Pluto drawn relatively far away? (Our solar system naturally divides into what astronomers call the inner planets and outer planets.)

✓ Kilometer Bar: Diameter of Our Solar System = **78 AU**.

Extension

Q. Bend two paper clips into short "poles" with "feet," and tape them to your desk 5.2 cm apart. Spindle a full sheet of scratch paper over them, with the poles well centered. Tie a 30 cm piece of thread into a 13.0 cm loop, and place it over both paper clip foci. Run a pencil around the string loop to draw an ellipse:

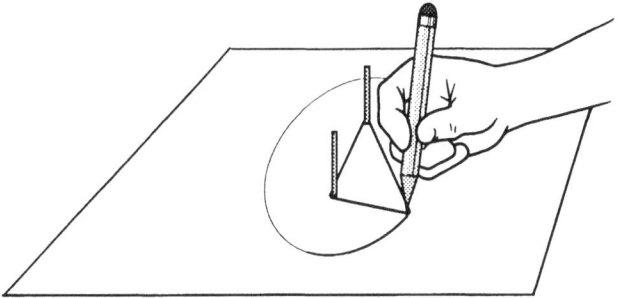

• This ellipse represents the actual shape of Pluto's orbit, with the sun at one of the paper clip focus points. Label Pluto's orbit and the sun's position.

• Neptune's orbit (like most of the planets) is *almost* a perfect circle. Draw Neptune's orbit to scale around the same sun position as Pluto. What can you discover?

A. If Pluto's scale distance from the sun is 13 cm, then Neptune's is 10 cm:
13 cm x 30 AU/39 AU = 10 cm.

Students should trace an orbit of this size to discover that Pluto is not always the outermost planet!

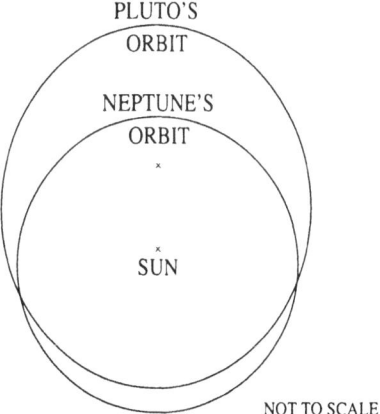

NOT TO SCALE

Materials

☐ The Sun Ruler cutout.
☐ Scissors.
☐ Clear tape.
☐ Masking tape.
☐ A straight pin.
☐ Two sheets of notebook paper.
☐ A lump of modeling clay.
☐ The Solar System Squares cutout.
☐ A pencil sharpener. Sharp pencils are needed in step 3c, and may need resharpening as students continue to draw each planet's orbit. Some may compensate for the pencil's increasing dullness by simply wiggling the pin in circles to ream out a larger hole.
☐ The Kilometer Bar.

Teaching Notes 13

THE PLANETS AND THE STARS ( )14

SKY SPHERE

1. Very carefully cut out both 6-gore patterns on a <u>North Stars</u> sheet as directed.
a. Tape these into a 12-gore circle so all lines match.

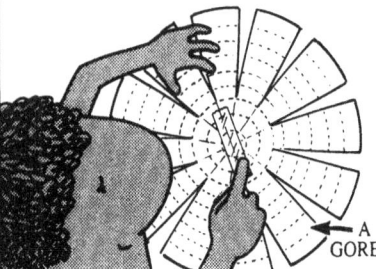
← A GORE

b. Label the back "N Stars."
c. Cut and tape a <u>South Stars</u> sheet in the same way. Label the back "S Stars."

2. Recall your home latitude to the nearest degree.
a. Count out from the center of each map this number of degrees. Make a pencil mark.

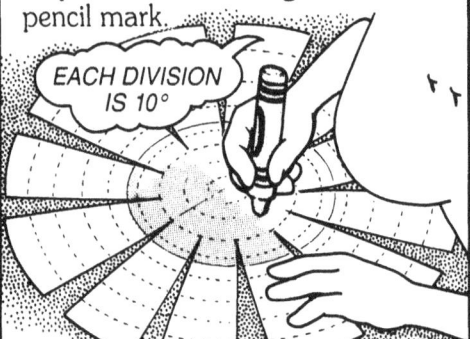
EACH DIVISION IS 10°

b. *Lightly* draw a circle with this radius around the center of each map. Color both circles yellow.

3. Window-trace Cassiopeia on the back side of the North Stars map and label it.

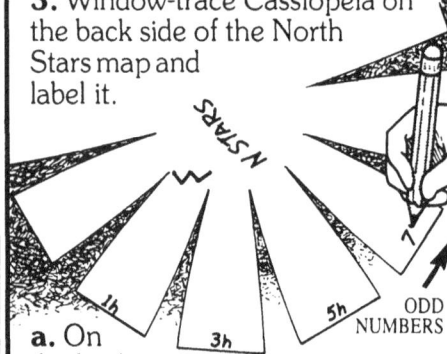
ODD NUMBERS

a. On the *back* of Cassiopeia's gore, write "1h" centered at the bottom edge.
b. Number all remaining gores to the *right* around the circle with *odd* numbers: 3h, 5h, ...to 23h.

4. Window-trace and label these constellations on the backs of both star maps. You'll need to jump gores as you draw.

• Big Dipper (12h, 55°N)
• Square of Pegasus (23.5h, 20°N)
• Leo (11h, 20°N)
• Orion (5.5h, 0°) – *don't miss bottom half on S map.*
• Scorpius (opposite Orion at 30°S) – *don't miss piece on next gore.*
• Southern Cross (2 gores clockwise of Scorpius on the *printed* side at 60°S).

5. Tape the 13h gore on the N map to the gore that holds the Southern Cross on the S map.

a. Window-trace the ecliptic from 0h (near Pegasus) across 12 gores in a giant S-shape.

b. Label the ecliptic <u>twice</u> as shown, writing one word on each gore:
ECLIPTIC — PATH OF SUN, PLANETS, MOON.

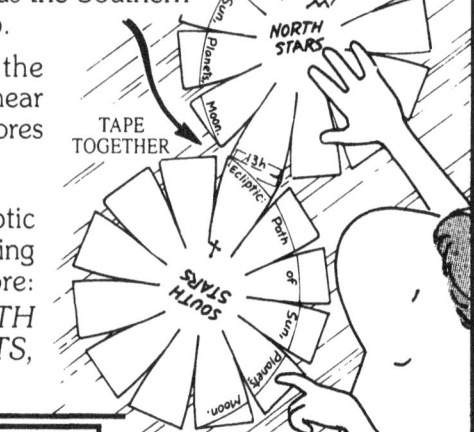
TAPE TOGETHER

6. Close the circles like a book, star maps to the inside.
a. Draw half-circles around these star hours: 7h, 15h, 23h.
b. Carefully join all gores with tape *except* those with circled hours. Fold the tape tightly around the ends so it *doesn't* stick out.

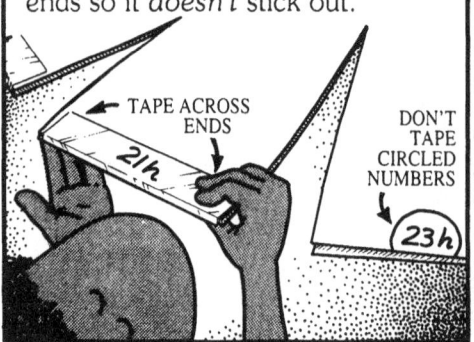
← TAPE ACROSS ENDS
DON'T TAPE CIRCLED NUMBERS

7. Carefully join the 3 circled gores, folding the tape so it *does* stick out.

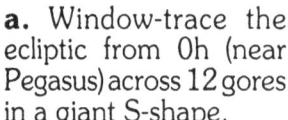
TAPE STICKS OUT
FOLD

a. Trim each folded edge, leaving a narrow lip of tape this wide:
b. *Gently* peel apart these tape strips from one side to the other.

8. Stick clear tape tabs on both sides of your Sky Sphere.

← TAB
SKY WINDOW!

9. Get the <u>Concept List</u> for this activity. Take turns reading each statement aloud, then demonstrating on your Sky Sphere that it is true. How many concepts did you both understand?

Copyright © 1994 by TOPS Learning Systems, Canby OR 97013. Reproduction limited to personal classroom use.

Objective

To assemble a paper globe that maps the constellations. To compare this model of the celestial sphere of previous models.

Lesson Notes

This Sky Sphere will be used to locate and identify constellations and planets in the night sky. Every student in your class should make one to use at home.

1. It takes about 20 minutes to cut and assemble both 12-gore circles. Remind students to cut *on* the lines, to the point of each "V" at the 60° circle (third ring from the center).

2. Students should start at the *center* of each sphere, as directed, and count outward the same number of degrees as their home latitude. In effect, they are locating a point on the sphere that is the *complement* of their home latitude (90° minus latitude).

Refer students who don't remember their home latitude back to their Pointer Boxes. Their stick figure is standing on top of it.

These yellow circles define the polar regions in the celestial sphere that are *always* visible and *never* visible at your particular north latitude. They will be studied in greater detail after the Sky Sphere is fully assembled.

3b. Even hours aren't shown because they are in the gaps between gores, equidistant from odd hours.

7. These 3 gores with circled hour numbers form "sky windows" for viewing the stars inside. Narrow lips of tape hold each window closed until you gently peel it open. To close the window again, simply press both hemispheres together.

9. Concept List (Guide to Oral Discussion):

1. Your Sky Sphere maps the same starry sky as your Star Jar: *All seven constellations on the Star Jar occupy the same relative positions on the Sky Sphere.*

2. The celestial equator on your Sky Sphere is the same as the celestial equator on your Star Jar: *Both equators divide these star maps into a north half and a south half; both equators are subdivided into 24 star hours.*

3. The ecliptic circle on your Sky Sphere is the same as the ecliptic circle on your Star Jar: *Both circles are north of the celestial equator for half a year and south for half a year; both are divided into 12 months.*

4. Find your window-tracing of Orion near 5h on the celestial equator. To see this constellation *inside* your Sky Sphere, look through the 15h window: *Students should first locate Orion on the outside of their Sky Sphere, then find it inside by looking through a window on the opposite side.*

5. Find your window-tracing of Pegasus near 23h. To see this constellation *inside* your Sky Sphere, look through either the 7h window or the 15h window: *Students should view Pegasus both outside and inside their Sky Sphere as directed.*

6. Locate the Big Dipper north of Leo inside your Sky Sphere. Merak and Dubhe (2 stars in the Dipper's cup) point to Polaris near the North Celestial Pole (NCP): *View the Big Dipper though the 23h window. Polaris, near the NCP, lies close to an extension of the line that connects Merak and Dubhe.*

7. Find the handle of the Big Dipper. Follow its arc to Arcturus (in Bootes), then continue along this curve to Spica (in Virgo): *Looking through the 23h window, students should follow the curve in the Dipper handle to locate each star in each constellation.*

8. Arcturus is N of the celestial equator in Bootes. Spica is S of the celestial equator in Virgo. These stars point to Crux (also called the Southern Cross) far to the south: *The Sky Sphere folds together at the celestial equator. Arcturus lies to the north of this fold and Spica to the south. These 2 stars define a great circle that passes reasonably close to the Southern Cross.*

9. The belt of Orion points north of the celestial equator toward Aldebaran (in Taurus) and south toward Sirius (in Canis Major): *Students can get the best view of Orion by looking through the 15h window. The 3 stars in his belt tilt NW toward Aldebaran and SE toward Sirius.*

10. Locate the Guardians of the Pole on your Polar Graph. Find these same 2 stars in Ursa Minor (also called the Little Dipper) in your Sky Sphere: *These stars are located at about 15 h and 73° N on both maps.*

11. Your Polar Graph maps part of the same sky as your Sky Sphere: *Look at the NCP through any window of the Sky Sphere to see the Big Dipper, Cassiopeia and 3 stars in the Little Dipper arranged around the NCP in the same pattern as on the Polar Graph.*

12. The sun's position is too far south to be plotted on the Polar Graph. The Sun Arrow can only point in its direction: *The summer solstice sun reaches as far north as 23.5° N. This falls far short of the 45° N limit of the Polar Graph.*

Answers

9. Students should count the total number of concepts they understand and write that number.

✓ <u>Sky Sphere</u>: Are both sides correctly marked N Stars and S Stars? Are the gores uniformly cut to the 60° circle? Do the windows open at 7h, 15h and 21h? Are equal areas of both Polar caps colored yellow? Are seven constellations (4 1/2 on the N side, 2 1/2 on the S side) traced and labeled? Does a labeled ecliptic circle cross 6 gores on the north side and 6 gores on the south?

Materials

☐ The North Stars and the South Stars cutouts.
☐ Scissors.
☐ Clear tape.
☐ A Pointer Box. This is an optional reference for those students who forget their home latitude.
☐ A yellow marker. This might be a crayon, pencil or marking pen.
☐ A window or light table suitable for make tracings.
☐ The Polar Graph from activity 9.
☐ The Star Jar from activity 6.

THE PLANETS AND THE STARS ( )15

THE ZODIAC

1. Cut out both <u>Sky Tabs</u>. Fold them into "W" shapes, then tape each one together at the middle.

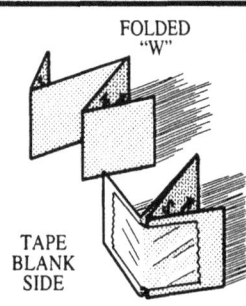

a. Roll masking tape sticky-side-out and stick it in the middle of a paper plate. Stick the SCP tab on top so it is perfectly centered.

b. Center the NCP tab on the *bottom* of a second paper plate in the same manner.

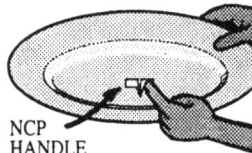

2. Hold your Sky Sphere against a window. Trace the dashed circle (onto both sides) where all cut marks end.

a. Stick 12 small rolls of masking tape along your table edge.

b. Stick them to the north side of your Sky Sphere, so each one rests *just* inside your traced circle, at the end of each cut.

3. Turn your NCP plate so its tab is underneath, on the table.

a. Lightly rest your Sky Sphere on the rim, taped side down.

b. Center it accurately, then press down to stick.

4. Stick 12 small rolls of tape to the south half of your Sky Sphere in the same way. Center the bottom of the SCP plate on top, and press the plates together.

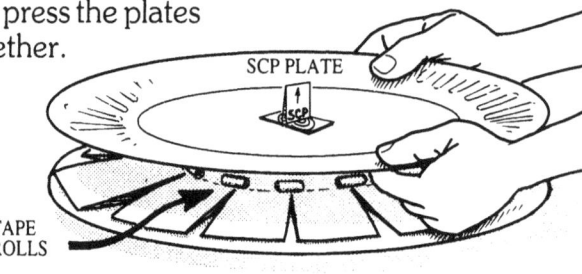

5. Cut out all 3 pieces of the <u>Zodiac Ring</u>. Arrange them in a circle so all 12 months are correctly ordered, then tape the ends *evenly* together to form a raised ring.

a. Lay this ring on the rim of your NCP plate so its sidereal hours match the hours you wrote on your Sky Map underneath. Center the ring so it doesn't overlap the plate edge, then tape it in this position.

b. Put a paper clip on the Zodiac Ring at your current calendar date to represent the sun. At what sidereal hour do you find the sun this time of year?

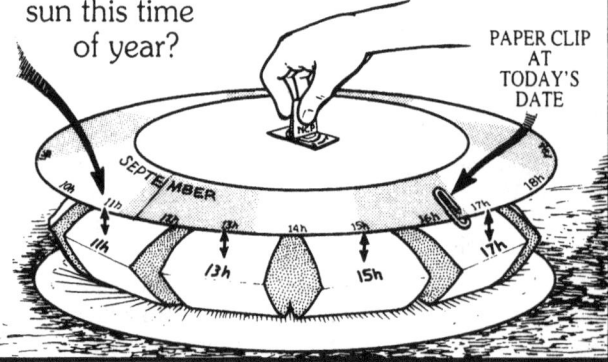

6. Each zodiac constellation named on the top plate is shown near the ecliptic circle inside your Sky Sphere. Find, draw and label all 12 constellations.

a. Name 3 bright stars (and 3 constellations) that define the *Summer Triangle*.
(Find these above the celestial equator at 20h.)

b. Name 7 bright stars (and 6 constellations) that define the *Winter Hexagon*.
(Find these near the celestial equator between 5h and 8h.)

Objective

To cap the Sky Sphere with a Zodiac Ring that fixes the sun's ecliptic position among the constellations in terms of calendar date and sidereal time.

Lesson Notes

1. It is important in activity 19 that these tabs be accurately centered. If your students are unable to do this visually, they can use gravity: nest 2 paper plates together and gently invert them over a pin point. Find the center of gravity where they balance level, then push the pins through both plates at this balance point to mark their centers.

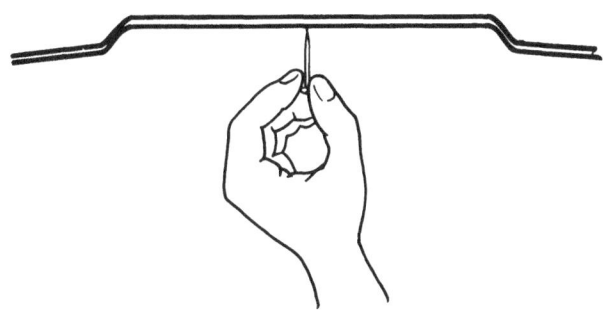

2a. Small, tight rolls of tape work best, because they can be placed most accurately at the end of each cut. An efficient way to produce these is to first roll 6 pieces of tape in the same direction that it peels off the roll. Then cut each roll in half to make 12 pieces.

Answers

✓ Sky Sphere (with Zodiac Ring): Is the NCP tab attached to the plate with the Zodiac Ring? Are both Sky Tabs accurately centered and firmly taped? Is the Zodiac Ring centered so it doesn't overlap the edge of the plate? Do the odd sidereal hours on the outside of the Zodiac Ring match the hours written on the N Star gores directly beneath? Is a paper clip fixed to the edge of the plate at the sun's current sidereal hour?

5b. Students should report the sidereal hour that corresponds to their current calendar date on the Zodiac Ring, then place a paper clip at that position.

6.

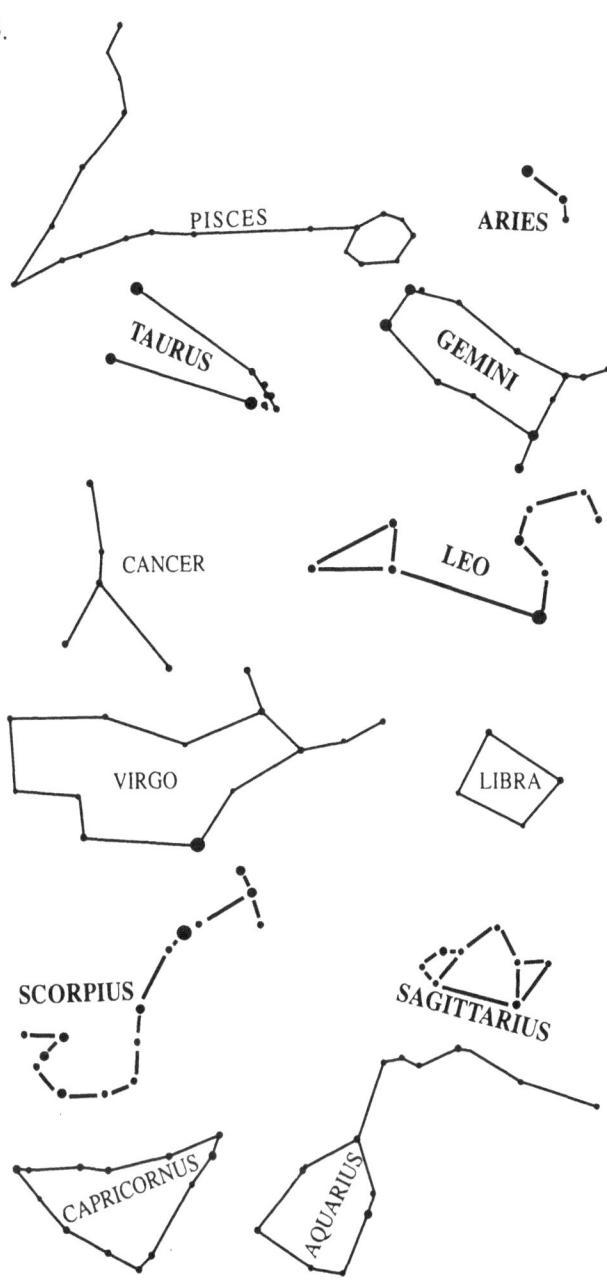

6a. Vega in LYRA
    Deneb in CYGNUS
    Altair in AQUILA

6b. Aldebaran in TAURUS
    Capella in AURIGA
    Castor and Pollux in GEMINI
    Procyon in CANIS MINOR
    Sirius in CANIS MAJOR
    Rigel in ORION

Materials

☐ The Sky Tabs cutout.
☐ Scissors
☐ Masking tape.
☐ Two paper plates. Use a standard 9 inch diameter with traditional rippled border.
☐ The Sky Sphere from activity 14.
☐ The Zodiac Ring cutout.
☐ Clear tape.
☐ A paper clip.

THE PLANETS AND THE STARS ( )16

STAR SEARCH

1. Imagine that a jet plane leaves a vapor trail that starts at Polaris, crosses your zenith, and disappears over your south horizon, heading straight for the SCP. This arc across the sky represents your *meridian*.

a. Trace your meridian across the room with your hand. Explain how you did this.

b. The sun and stars always *culminate* (reach their highest point in the sky) when they cross your meridian. When does the sun cross your meridian?

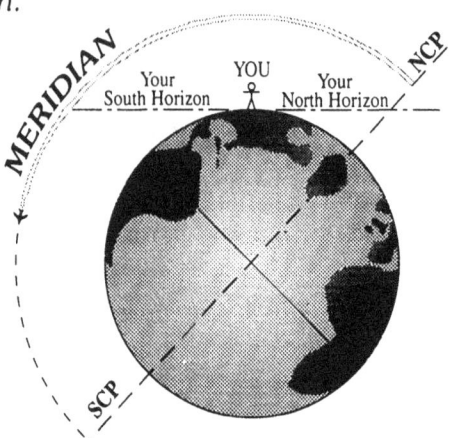

2. Get your Sky Sphere and a Concept List for this activity. Take turns reading each statement aloud, then demonstrate with your Sky Sphere that it is true. How many concepts did you both understand?

TURN THIS DIRECTION

3. Get a Sky Dictionary sheet.

a. List 21 important constellations (printed in bold) and their meanings.

b. Practice pronouncing each name in this list until you can say it correctly.

kas′ē-o-pē′yah

4. Trim off the outer margin on a Sky Wheel sheet. Tape your Sky Dictionary behind it at the corner stamp labeled "Vulpecula."

a. Cut out stamps for the constellations that you have already seen in the night sky. Copy information you recorded below your Polar Graph onto each stamp.

b. Tape each stamp to your Sky Wheel at the same sidereal hour and declination as on your Sky Sphere.

CONSTELLATION	
Write the ORDER of your discovery here.	Write the DATE of your discovery here.
	Write the HOUR of your discovery (with a.m./p.m.) here.

5. Paper-punch a "sun" from masking tape. Stick it to the ecliptic circle on your Sky Wheel at the sun's current sidereal hour.

TAPE "SUN"

a. Will you be able to find new constellations at night near this model sun? Explain.

b. Will you need to update the position of this paper-punch "sun" from time to time? Why?

c. As you add stamps to your Sky Wheel, you are making a star map. Explain how to position it against the sky.

6. Take your Sky Sphere home over the next few weeks. Use it to explore the night sky.

• Each time you find a new constellation, fill in its stamp and add it to your Sky Wheel. Use the Sky Dictionary to pronounce each name correctly and understand its meaning.

• To light up your Sky Sphere in the dark, tape your flashlight under the SCP plate.

• You will use your Sky Sphere again to complete activity 19. Remember to bring it back to class.

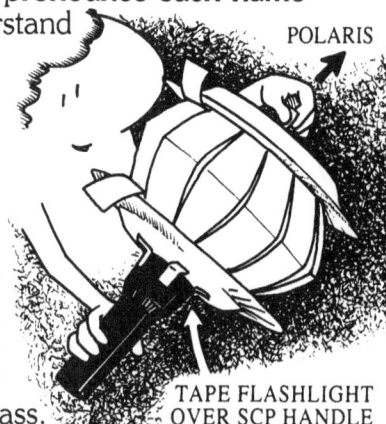

TAPE FLASHLIGHT OVER SCP HANDLE

Copyright © 1994 by TOPS Learning Systems, Canby OR 97013. Reproduction limited to personal classroom use.

Objective

To search out constellations in the night sky over the next few weeks and record them on a Sky Wheel.

Supporting Concepts

◐ Distribute the photocopied Sky Dictionary. Pronounce each bold constellation name for your students, then together as a class, until they become familiar with the accent marks and long vowel sounds.

Lesson Notes

2. <u>Concept List (Guide to Oral Discussion)</u>:

1. Rotate your Sky Sphere so Orion rises due east, crosses your meridian, and sets due west. Meanwhile, Polaris hardly moves at all: *Point the NCP tab at Polaris while turning the Sky Sphere in the direction of the arrows on either tab. Orion circles as indicated, while Polaris rotates almost in place.*

2. As Orion culminates at your *meridian*, Leo rises to your east and Pegasus sets to your west: *Point the NCP tab at Polaris while turning Orion to its highest point. In this position, Leo and Pegasus rise and set as described.*

3. Hold the Sky Sphere over your head so you can look *inside* the sphere to see Orion crossing your meridian: *Hold the Sky Sphere overhead while pointing the NCP tab at Polaris. Turn it east to west until you see Orion through the 15 h window.*

4. Look *inside* your sky sphere to see Orion, Auriga and Lepus all cross your meridian at the same time: *Hold the sky sphere overhead, tilted toward Polaris, while looking up through the 15h window. All 3 constellations cross your meridian together, Auriga above Orion's head and Lepus under Orion's feet.*

5. Perseus, Auriga and Gemini move across my meridian in that order: *Hold the Sky Sphere overhead tilted toward Polaris. Slowly turn it east to west while looking through the 15h window.*

6. Pegasus, Andromeda and Perseus move across my meridian in that order: *Hold the Sky Sphere overhead tilted toward Polaris. Slowly turn it E to W while looking through the 15h window.*

7. Scorpius, Sagittarius and Capricornus move across my meridian in that order. I see these looking both inside and outside the Sky Sphere: *See these inside by holding the Sky Sphere overhead in the correct orientation while looking through the 7h window. Lower the tilted Sky Sphere to see these same constellations outside on the Zodiac Ring.*

8. As I tilt the Sky Sphere toward Polaris and turn it from east to west, all stars in the yellow NCP circle go round and round but never set: *This yellow circle just touches my northern horizon, but no part of it dips lower.*

9. As I tilt the Sky Sphere toward Polaris and turn it from east to west, all stars in the yellow SCP circle go round and round but never rise: *This yellow circle just touches my southern horizon, but no part of it rises higher.*

10. Cassiopeia always circles *above* your horizon; the Southern Cross always circles *below* your horizon; Orion circles equally above and below your horizon: *Cassiopeia is in the yellow NCP circle; the Southern Cross is in the yellow SCP circle; Orion is midway between these yellow circles on the celestial equator.*

11. In June, the sun reaches its most northerly summer position as it leaves the constellation Taurus and moves into Gemini. This is a bad time of year to see Orion, but a good time of year to see Scorpius: *The sun reaches its summer solstice position on the ecliptic between these two zodiac constellations. Nearby Orion is lost in the glare of the sun, but Scorpius on the opposite side of the Sky Sphere culminates at midnight.*

12. In March, the sun leaves Aquarius, passing northward across the celestial equator into Pisces. This is a bad time of year to see Pegasus, but a good time of year to see Leo: *The sun reaches is spring equinox position between these two zodiac constellations. Nearby Pegasus is lost in the glare of the sun, but Leo on the opposite side of the Sky Sphere culminates at midnight.*

4a. Students who have not yet made any star observations since activity 9 should place at least one stamp to become familiar with this process. Allow them 1 stamp "on credit." They should write a number 1 next to a constellation they "know" they'll spot first, then fill in its date and hour on the next clear night.

6. The flashlight must always be supported by one hand. To open a sky window with your other free hand, simply point the flashlight downward until gravity expands the Sky Sphere.

Answers

1a. Begin tracing your meridian at the NCP near Polaris. This is where the Polaris Straw points on your properly aligned Pointer Box. Sweep your hand up through your zenith, then down to your south horizon.

1b. The sun crosses your meridian at high noon.

2. Students should count the total number of concepts they understand and write that number.

3a. ANDROMEDA: Chained Maiden
AQUILA: Eagle	GRUS: Crane
ARIES: Ram	LEO: Lion
AURIGA: Charioteer	LYRA: Lyre
CANIS MAJOR: Big Dog	ORION: The Hunter
CANIS MINOR: Little Dog	PEGASUS: Winged Horse
CASSIOPEIA: Queen	PERSEUS: Hero
CORVUS: Crow	SAGITTARIUS: Archer
CRUX: Southern Cross	SCORPIUS: Scorpion
CYGNUS: Swan	TAURUS: Bull
GEMINI: Twins	URSA MAJOR: Great Bear

5a. No. Constellations near this "sun" punch will be lost in its glare. (Those a little farther removed might be seen low in the west after sunset, or low in the east before sunrise.)

5b. Yes. As the earth orbits the sun, the sun appears to move along the ecliptic into new background constellations. (About every 15 days it appears to advance 1 sidereal hour:
15 days/hour x 24 hours = 360 days ≈ 1 year.)

5c. Use this Sky Wheel just like the Polar Graph. Point its NCP (the 90° N position) at Polaris. Rotate it so the paper punch sun corresponds to the current position of the sun in the sky. The relative positions of all constellations stamps now corresponds to their current sky positions.

✓ <u>Sky Wheel</u>: Is the paper-punch "sun" applied to the ecliptic circle at the sun's current sidereal hour? (Find this star time on the Zodiac Ring or Star Jar.) Is at least 1 stamp correctly applied? Do your students understand how to fill in and place new stamps as they discover new constellations at home?

Materials

☐ Pointer Box (optional).
☐ The Concept List for this activity.
☐ The Sky Sphere from activity 15.
☐ The Sky Dictionary sheet.
☐ The Sky Wheel sheet.
☐ Scissors.
☐ Clear tape.
☐ The Polar Graph from activity 9.
☐ A paper punch tool.
☐ Masking tape.

THE PLANETS AND THE STARS ( )17

PROPORTIONAL PLANETS

1. Our Earth has a diameter of about 12,800 kilometers. This length is called one Earth Diameter (1 ED).

EARTH 12,800 k = 1 ED

a. Record this distance on your Kilometer Bar.

b. Get your Solar System Squares and find the diameter of Jupiter in ED. Calculate its diameter to the nearest thousand kilometers and mark this distance on your Kilometer Bar.

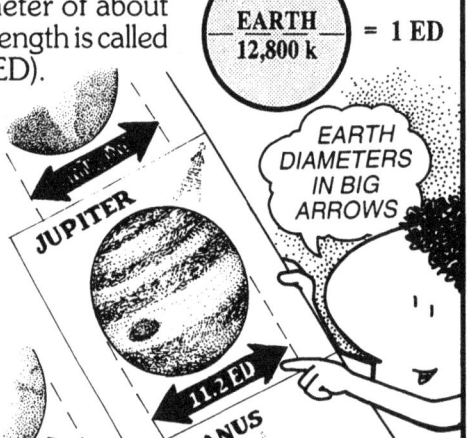

EARTH DIAMETERS IN BIG ARROWS

2. Cut out the Earth Ruler around the dashed line. Back all of it with masking tape, then *carefully* trim to the solid line.

CUT OUT FIRST...
...THEN TAPE THE BACK...
...THEN DO A FINAL TRIM.

3. Fold notebook paper in half the long way. Open it with the holes at the bottom, heading to the left.

a. Read the *diameter* of Mercury at the *bottom* of its square in ED. How many tiny units on your Earth Ruler equal this diameter?

b. Draws a line equal to Mercury's diameter where the fold crosses the first line on the left. Draw a circle around it and label this "planet" Mercury.

c. Use your Earth Ruler to draw Venus, Earth and Mars right next to each other along the fold line. Label each circle.

4. Draw and label Jupiter, Saturn, Uranus and Neptune like this:

a. Draw each planet's diameter on the fold and locate its center with your Earth Ruler.

b. Set a compass on this center over a square of masking tape stuck to your table.

c. Turn the compass with one hand to draw each planet's circumference.

5. Draw and label tiny Pluto freehand.

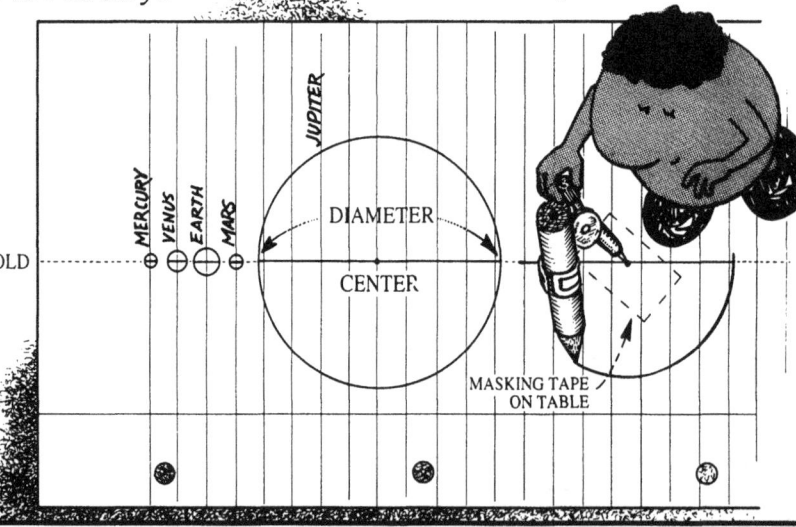

6. How many ED's are in a Sun Diameter? Measure out this many ED's in thread. Show your math.

a. Lightly tape your notebook paper to the table.

b. Fold the thread in half. Use this as a radius to draw and label part of the sun's curve at the far left.

THE THREAD MAKES A BIG COMPASS!
HALF THE DIAMETER IS THE RADIUS.
LABEL THE SUN'S CURVE.

5. Add details, as on your Solar System Squares, to make each planet look realistic.

Copyright © 1994 by TOPS Learning Systems, Canby OR 97013. Reproduction limited to personal classroom use.

Objective

To draw the sizes of the sun and the planets to scale on a piece of notebook paper.

Supporting Concepts

◊ Demonstrate the correct use of a drawing compass.
• Set the point of a compass on a soft surface (like a piece of masking tape) where it will not slip.
• Twist the top of the compass between the thumb and index finger of one hand.

Lesson Notes

2. Backing the ruler with masking tape gives it enough substance to be used as a straightedge for drawing planet diameters in steps 3-5.

3-4. Leave only a millimeter or two of space between planets so you don't run out of room at the other end of the paper.

Extension

Q. Choose one of your 10 Solar System Squares to study in depth. Do research in the library and write a report.

Answers

1b. Jupiter's diameter is 11.2 times larger than Earth's diameter: 12,800 k/ED x 11.2 ED = 143,000 k

3a. Four tiny units on the Earth Ruler equal the 0.4 ED diameter of Mercury.

6. The Sun Square lists 108 ED as the diameter of the sun:
   1 ruler/12 ED x 108 ED = 9 rulers
Students should measure out a length of thread equal to 9 rulers to model the sun's scale diameter.

✓ <u>Kilometer Bar</u>: Student responses are listed in bold.
Diameter of Jupiter = **143,000 k**
One Earth Diameter (1 ED) = **12,800 k**

✓ <u>Proportional Planets Drawing</u>: Are the planets and sun sized similar to the notebook paper illustration in step 6? Are they correctly labeled?

Materials

☐ The Kilometer Bar.
☐ The Solar System Squares.
☐ The Earth Ruler cutout.
☐ Scissors.
☐ Masking tape.
☐ Notebook paper.
☐ A drawing compass.
☐ Thread.

---

6. <u>Concept List</u> (Guide to Oral Discussion for lesson 19):

1. The sun, moon, planets and stars all appear to turn full circle on a daily basis, with you at the center: *Point the NCP tab at Polaris while turning the expanded Sky Sphere in the direction of the arrows on the SCP tab. Imagine yourself at the center of the sphere, watching all these celestial bodies circle from horizon to horizon.*
2. A planet at eastern quadrature seems to *follow* the sun in its daily journey across the sky. A planet at western quadrature seems to *lead* the sun: *Turn the Sky Sphere in the direction of the arrows on the SCP tab. The eastern quadrature label circles behind the sun, while the western quadrature label circles ahead of it.*
3. A first quarter moon is at eastern quadrature: it seems to *follow* the sun in its daily journey across the sky. A third quarter moon is at western quadrature: it seems to *lead* the sun: *These moons, and the labels next to them, seem to follow and lead the sun, respectively, as you turn the Sky Sphere from east to west.*
4. Turn your paper clip "sun" to its midnight position. The tape tags on the ecliptic circle now show where to find the moon and planets <u>at midnight</u>: *Point the NCP tab at Polaris with the sun marker at its lowest position. All tags on the ecliptic circle now correspond to the actual positions of the celestial bodies above or below your horizon at midnight.*
5. Turn your paper clip "sun" so it is setting in the west. The tape tags on the ecliptic circle now show where to find the moon and planets <u>at sunset</u>: *Point the NCP tab at Polaris with the sun marker pointing westward to the setting position of today's sun. (This is south of west when the sun is low on its ecliptic circle, and north of west when the sun is high.) All tags on the ecliptic circle now correspond to the actual positions of the celestial bodies above or below your horizon at sunset.*
6. Turn your paper clip "sun" to its current position in your sky. The tape tags on the ecliptic circle show where to find the moon and planets <u>right now</u>: *Point the NCP tab at Polaris with the sun marker pointing to the sun's current position. All tags on the ecliptic circle now correspond to the actual positions of the celestial bodies above or below your horizon right now. (If the moon is near either quadrature confirm that it is accurately placed. Look for it in the daytime sky right now!)*

7. The word "planet" comes from a Greek word meaning "wanderer." These planets are so named because they appear to move from month to month against a fixed background of zodiac constellations: *The arrows associated with each planet show their actual eastward shift among the zodiac constellations.*
8. Mercury takes about 3 months to orbit the sun; Venus takes about 7 months; Mars takes about 22 months: *The length of each planet arrow shows how far it moves in one earth month. About 3 Mercury arrows fit into that orbit, about 7 Venus arrows fit into the that orbit, and about 22 Mars arrows fit into that orbit.*
9. Mercury and Venus always appear close to the sun. They never appear in opposition like Mars, Jupiter and Saturn: *Because Mercury and Venus orbit between the earth and sun, they never move "behind" the earth like Mars, Jupiter and Saturn.*
10. During eastern elongation, Venus is commonly called the evening "star." During western elongation it is known as the morning "star:" *Venus follows the sun during eastern elongation, setting in the evening after the sun sets. Venus leads the sun during western elongation, rising in the morning before the sun rises.*
11. The moon appears to circle westward once a day, while it drifts eastward in a full circle once a month: *The moon appears to circle westward because the earth rotates. Model this by turning the sky sphere westward. While this is happening on a daily basis, the moon orbits eastward from new moon to new moon on a monthly basis. Model this by finger-tracing the moon's orbit drawn around the earth.*
12. The sun appears to circle westward once a day, while it drifts eastward in a full circle once a year: *The sun appears to circle westward because the earth rotates. Model this by turning the sky sphere westward. While this is happening on a daily basis, the earth moves full circle around the sun on a yearly basis. Model this by finger-tracing the advancing calendar dates counterclockwise around the Zodiac. (Imagine moving the earth off center in a counterclockwise direction, as suggested by the earth orbit arrows printed on the Planet Finder. Notice how this brings the sun into new alignments with advancing calendar dates.)*

(Teaching Notes 19 continued)

THE PLANETS AND THE STARS ( )18
ELBOW ROOM

1. Get your Solar System Squares. Are the sun and planets on these squares drawn to scale? Explain.

2. Find a dark speck of pepper with a diameter of about 0.6 mm. Imagine how big *you* would be standing on an *earth* this size!

a. Stick this speck on the *back* of your Earth square with clear tape. Label it.

b. If the earth is a 0.6 mm pepper-grain, what is the diameter of Jupiter at this scale? Tape a pebble of this diameter to the back of the Jupiter square and label it.

c. Choose other pepper specks or pebbles that correctly proportion the rest of the planets. Show your math as necessary.

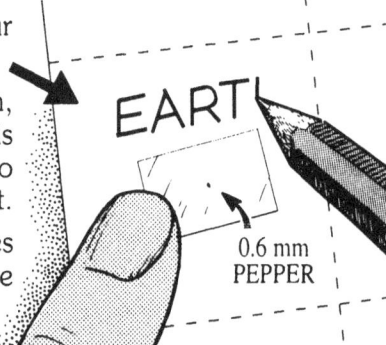

3. If the earth is a 0.6 mm pepper grain, how many mm across is the sun? Does a tennis ball have the correct diameter?

4. Your Sun Square lists 1 AU (the distance from the sun to the earth) as equal to 108 sun diameters.

a. If a tennis ball "sun" has a diameter of 6.5 cm, how many centimeters separate it from a pepper-grain earth?

b. How many meters is this?

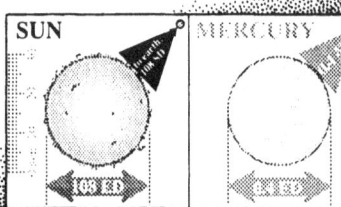

5. While sitting, tape a 50 cm piece of string to your knees with strips of masking tape 15 cm long. Taping over bare skin or pant legs is OK.

a. Fold back each end of the string and tape it again with another short strip over each long one.

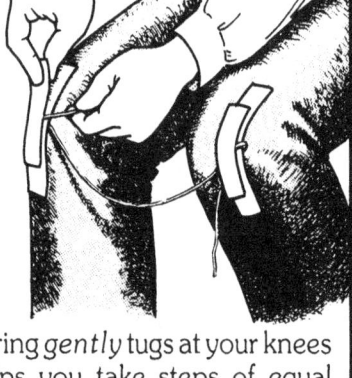

b. Walk normally so the string *gently* tugs at your knees with each step. This helps you take steps of equal length.

c. Mark a distance of 7 meters (1 AU to scale) on the floor. By trial and error, adjust the length of string joining your knees until 10 equal paces always carry you 7 meters.

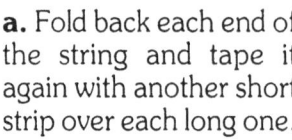

d. When you find the correct length, reinforce each end with extra tape. With gentle knee tugs as your guide, you now walk in measured paces of 1/10 AU.

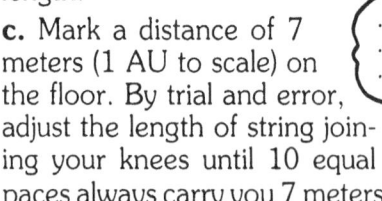

6. Cut apart all planet squares. Keep them in order.

a. Go outside and lay out your model solar system to scale. Walk in 0.1 AU paces, starting from a tennis-ball sun!

b. Lay squares all the way to Pluto, if possible.

7. Think of all horizon objects beyond your tennis-ball "sun" as background stars in the zodiac constellations.

a. As you walk to the right (all the planets orbit counterclockwise) which way does the "sun" appear to shift in this zodiac "star field?"

b. The sun is now "in" constellation **Y** as shown. Where was it before? Where is it headed?

8. Look around at your "sun, planets and stars." Everything is to scale as you would see it in space. Write your impressions.

Objective

To model the sizes of the planets and their distances from the sun in the same scale model. To appreciate that our solar system is a very empty place.

Supporting Concepts

✪ Set a chair on a desk in the middle of your room and rest a tennis ball "sun" on the seat. Find a pepper-speck "earth" about 0.6 mm in diameter and tape it to an index card. Hold these 7 meters apart. Our earth-sun system reduced 21.4 billion times has these proportions.

✪ Orbit the pepper-speck counterclockwise around the tennis ball (like the real earth around the real sun). Describe how this sun appears to move in front of different objects in your classroom (like the real sun among the background stars of the zodiac.)

Lesson Notes

2. Students should choose dark pepper specks or pebbles that easily show up against a white paper background. Secure the Jupiter pebble with just one layer of clear tape to preserve a clear view through the tape.

3. Parallax makes this measurement smaller than the ball really is. Measuring at full arm's length reduces this error.

5. Folding the string back on itself prevents it from slipping. To adjust its length, temporarily peel up the short tape on either side, then pull on the string to lengthen or shorten.

6. If necessary, lay out the first 3 planets inside your classroom to demonstrate the procedure your students will follow outside:
• Set the "sun" on the floor at one side of your room.
• Pretend your knees are joined with string to measure out 0.1 AU paces. Count 4 paces from the sun (0.1, 0.2, 0.3, 0.4 AU) then set the Mercury Square, pepper speck up, at this distance
• Continue counting paces to Venus (0.5, 0.6, 0.7 AU) and place the Venus Square. Remind students that you are reading AU's on each square, not ED's.
• Continue counting paces to Earth (0.8, 0.9, 1.0 AU) and place the Earth Square. Outside, your students will pace and place planet squares as far as space permits. At 390 tenth-AU paces (273 meters or 300 yards), Pluto may be too remote to place.

✓ Solar System Squares: Is a pepper speck or pebble of the correct size taped to the back of each square?

Answers

1. No. The real sun and real planets have dramatically different sizes. These Solar System Squares show them all with the same size.

2b. Jupiter, at 11.2 ED, is 11.2 times farther across than the 0.6 mm earth speck:

Jupiter = 11.2 × 0.6 mm ≈ 6.7 mm.

Students should look for a round pebble that approximately equals this size, and tape it to the back of the Jupiter square.

2c. Once the earth speck is taped in place, students can use it as a standard of comparison to "eyeball" other planet specks for the correct size. Math is optional.

Mercury = 0.4 ED, a little less than half the earth speck:
0.4 × 0.6mm ≈ 0.2mm
Venus = 0.9 ED, almost same size as the earth speck:
0.9 × 0.6mm ≈ 0.5 mm
Mars = 0.5 ED, half the earth speck:
0.5 × 0.6mm ≈ 0.3 mm
Pluto = 0.2 ED, a fifth as wide as the earth speck:
0.2 ED × 0.6 mm ≈ 0.1 mm

These remaining 3 planets, like Jupiter, require pebbles. Multiplication and direct measurement (with the Sun Square's ruler) are useful.

Saturn = 9.4 ED: 9.4 × 0.6mm ≈ 5.6 mm
Uranus = 4.0 ED: 4.0 × 0.6mm ≈ 2.4 mm
Neptune = 3.8 ED: 3.8 × 0.6mm ≈ 2.3 mm

3. Sun diameter = 108 earth diameters (ED):
108 ED × 0.6 mm/ED = 64.8 mm ≈ 6.5 cm
This is very close to the size of a tennis ball.

4a. Earth-sun distance = 108 sun diameters (SD):
1 AU = 108 SD × 6.5 cm/SD = 702 cm

4b. 702 cm ≈ 7 meters

7a. As you walk right, the "sun" appears to shift left in front of the "background stars."

7b. The sun was in constellation **Z**. As you continue to orbit, it will appear to move into constellation **X**.

8. Seen in its true scale, our solar system is a remarkably empty place. The sun and planets add up to a mere sprinkling of matter scattered across a field of nothing.

(The void beyond our solar system contains even less matter. At the scale of this model we must travel another 200 kilometers before arriving at another vacant field containing two tennis balls and a plum. This is the triple star system of our nearest neighbor, Alpha Centauri. It may or may not have planets. At 200 kilometers, a pepper speck is very difficult to see.)

Materials

☐ Solar System Squares.
☐ Ground black pepper.
☐ Clear tape.
☐ A container of coarse sand with pebbles.
☐ A tennis ball.
☐ A meter stick.
☐ Heavy string.
☐ Masking tape.
☐ Scissors.
☐ Clothespins (optional). These are convenient for keeping the solar squares in order after they are cut apart in step 6. If it is windy, they can be used outside to anchor the squares.

THE WANDERERS

1. Cut around the Planet Finder (and its notch.) Cut out the grey circle in the center.

a. Fit this hole over the NCP tab of your Sky Sphere.

b. Stick a folded tab of clear tape over the Sun Notch. Make it stick out far enough to slide under the paper clip at today's calendar date.

2. Jupiter moves 1 arrow length (on average) around the sun each month. Make a small flat planet marker from clay and set it in front of an arrow on Jupiter's orbit.

a. Move this marker around the sun in the direction of Jupiter's arrows. Stop at the black "signpost" labeled Eastern Quadrature. Draw how Jupiter lines up with the earth and sun, like this:

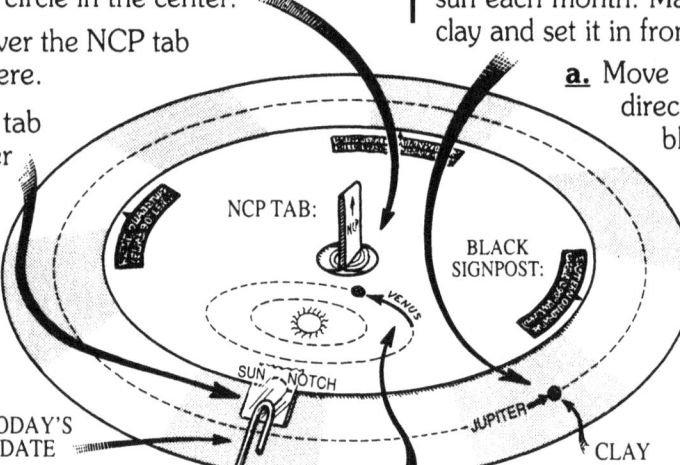

EASTERN QUADRATURE: Jupiter and Sun at right angle to Earth.

3. Venus moves 1 arrow length (on average) around the sun each month. Set your clay marker in front of the Venus arrow.

a. Move this clay marker around the sun in the direction of the Venus arrow.

b. As you pass each grey "signpost," draw and label circles to show how Venus lines up with the earth and sun.

b. Move to the other 3 black "signposts" and make similar diagrams. Each should describe, in words and pictures, how Jupiter lines up with the earth and sun.

4. Cut a strip of masking tape this long: Fold the sticky side together lengthwise, leaving a third of the tape exposed. Stick it to your table.

a. Use a pen to list each of these names *twice* on the tape in neat bold letters: MOON, MERC, VEN, MARS, JUP, SAT.

b. Cut between each name to make tags. Stick them to your table.

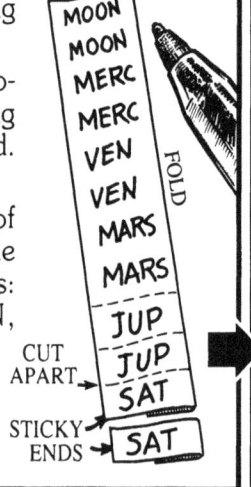

5. Get a Celestial Events sheet.

a. Read about each planet's current sky position for your current month. Stick a planet tag on each orbit where you think it belongs.

b. Use the Celestial Events sheet or a calendar to tag the current location of the moon as it orbits the earth. (From one new moon to the next takes about 4 weeks.)

c. Stick a second set of tags to the Ecliptic Circle on the outside of the gores. Position each tag directly under its duplicate on the plate.

PLACE PLANET & MOON TAGS

PLACE MATCHING TAGS ON ECLIPTIC CIRCLE

6. Get a Concept Sheet for this activity. Take turns reading each statement and demonstrating it with your Sky Sphere. How many did you both understand?

7. Try to find a planet in the night sky and sketch its position relative to nearby background stars. As you observe this planet from week to week, how does it move among these stars?

Objective

To track the planets and the moon on the ecliptic circle. To visually identify at least one planet and document its shifting position among the background stars.

Supporting Concepts

✪ Stretch out your *right* hand, palm *out*, fingers spread. Let your index finger represent the sun, flanked by the planet "Thumb" on your left and the planet "Pinky" on your right. Stand with your students facing south. Ask everyone to move their right hands, palms *always* out, to track these bodies across the sky from east to west.
• Which planet is in the Western position? (Pinky) The Eastern position? (Thumb)
• Which planet "leads" the sun? (Pinky) "Follows" the sun? (Thumb)
• Which planet sets first? (Pinky) Rises first? (Pinky)
• Which planet do you see after sunset? (Thumb) Before sunrise? (Pinky)

✪ Hold one hand in a "thumbs up" position to represent a planet; the other hand palm open to represent the sun. Your head represents the earth. Ask everyone to slowly turn clockwise while observing their thumb planet and palm sun at these positions:
• Opposition: hold the planet and sun on *opposite sides* of your head.
• Conjunction: hold the planet and sun on *the same side* of your head. If the planet is in front of the sun this is an Inferior Conjunction; if the planet is in back of the sun this is a Superior Conjunction.
• Western Quadrature: hold your arms at a right angle with the thumb planet leading the palm sun as you turn.
• Eastern Quadrature: hold your arms at a right angle with the thumb planet following the palm sun as you turn. (Changing from one quadrature to the other involves switching the planet and sun to the opposite hand.)

Lesson Notes

2-3. Even though each planet's arrow models the actual monthly advance of that planet around the sun, this does not necessarily equal the shift we apparently see among the zodiac stars. This is because we watch the planets from a moving platform, namely the earth. Imagine watching joggers run around a track while you yourself run around the same track. Those running opposite you on the far side of the track seem to whiz past background objects quickly. Those running with you on the same side of the track seem to pass background objects slowly. If you overtake these runners very quickly on the inside, they even "retrograde" (move backward against background objects). These effects are easily demonstrated on a sun-centered model of the solar system, but not on this earth-centered Planet Finder.

Observing our solar system from an orbiting earth, we must regard these planet arrows as representing an *average* monthly advance through the zodiac. One year from now, when the earth returns to where it is now, find each planet 12 arrows farther along. The speedups, slowdowns and retrogrades due to parallax have all averaged out.

5. Don't expect your students to accurately place all of these planet tags on their first attempt. As they compare their work with each other or make observations in the night sky, they'll have many occasions for self correction. These tags track a dynamic system. They are meant to be moved.

6. Concept List (Guide to Oral Discussion): Please turn to the bottom of teaching notes 17.

Answers

2-3. (All these descriptions imply an earth perspective.)

Eastern Quadrature: Jupiter and Sun at right angle. (E)(J)(S)

Opposition: Jupiter opposite Sun. (J)(E)(S)

Western Quadrature: Jupiter and Sun at right angle. (J)(E)(S)

Conjunction: Jupiter lined up with Sun. (E)(S)(J)

Maximum Eastern Elongation: Venus at widest separation from Sun. (E)(S)(V)

Inferior Conjunction: Venus in front of Sun. (E)(V)(S)

Maximum Western Elongation: Venus at widest separation from Sun. (E)(V)(S)

Superior Conjunction: Venus in back of Sun. (E)(S)(V)

6. Students should count the total number of concepts they understand and write that number.

7. This question can only be answered over a period of weeks by disciplined sky observes. Students who supply answers documented with star sketches should be awarded kudos and extra credit.

✓ Sky Sphere with Planet Finder: Is the Planet Finder centered on the Zodiac Circle? (Reposition the NCP tab as necessary.) Is it secured by a clear-tape tab at your current calendar date? Are planet and moon tabs on top of the plate lined up with corresponding tabs on the ecliptic circle beneath?

Extension.

Q. Check the accuracy of each planet position by reading the almanac back to the previous month and ahead to the next month. Remember to adjust the Sun Notch backward or forward among the calendar dates to match the time period you are reading about.

Materials

☐ The Planet Finder cutout.
☐ Scissors and a pen.
☐ The Sky Sphere with a paper clip marking the sun's current sidereal time.
☐ Clear tape and masking tape.
☐ Clay.
☐ A Celestial Events sheet. Borrow a current copy of The World Almanac and Book of Facts (or other almanac) from your library. Under Astronomy — Celestial Calendar, (or a similar heading) find a monthly summary of planet positions. Supply an information sheet that includes last month, this month and next month, or a copy of the book itself.
☐ A current calendar with moon phase information (optional). Moon positions might also be inferred from your almanac source, or by direct observation.
☐ The Concept Sheet for this activity.

THE PLANETS AND THE STARS ( )20

OUR MILKY WAY

1. Our sun and about 200 billion other stars are pulled by gravity into a slowly spinning *galaxy* called the Milky Way. Cut out the <u>Milky Way Disk</u> that models our home galaxy.

a. Pull apart a pinch of cotton into a super-thin layer. Cover your model galaxy with this thin film of "star dust." Stick it in place with rolled clear tape.

b. Stick an extra fluff of cotton in the middle. This models the center of our Milky Way, which is thicker than its edges.

Really thin cotton... gaps are OK.

2. Poke a pinhole at the center of the circle labeled "THIS SPACE MAPPED BY SKY SPHERE." From our sun at the center to the edge of this circle is 1,000 LY.

a. Record this distance on your Kilometer Bar. All but a few star on your Sky Sphere are closer than this!

b. The radius of the tiny pinhole itself is about 150 LY, with our sun at the center. Are Dubhe and Alkaid on your Dipper Box located inside this pinhole? Explain.

3. Insert a "pin person" into the pinhole up to its "neck." Imagine that you are looking around at the stars just like this pin person.

a. Would you expect to see more stars in one part of the sky than in another? Explain.

b. When you look between Scorpius and Sagittarius in our night Sky you are gazing into the *center* of our Galaxy. How are these vast numbers of stars shown on your Sky Sphere?

c. Trace the Milky Way full circle around your Sky Sphere. What shape does its soft light take in our night sky? Why?

Imagine you are here! MILKY WAY

BILLIONS OF "STARS"

4. Cut out the <u>Galaxy Ruler</u>. Measure the diameter of your model Milky Way. Mark this distance on your Kilometer Bar.

a. Andromeda, the nearest galaxy like our own, is 2,200,000 light years away. Mark this distance on your Kilometer Bar.

b. How many Galaxy Rulers span the distance between our Milky Way and Andromeda?

c. Use a paper plate to model Andromeda at the correct scale distance from our Milky Way. Explain how you did this.

2,200,000 LY

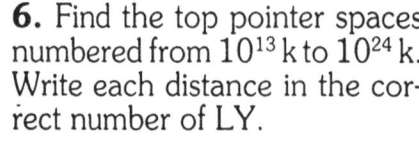
MILKY WAY GALAXY — ANDROMEDA GALAXY

5. These are only 2 of perhaps 100 *billion* galaxies scattered vast distances through our universe. Mark these distances on your Kilometer Bar:

a. The most distant galaxy ever detected by telescope is from 5 to 10 billion LY away.

b. Astronomers believe our *universe* (space and everything in it) extends 10 to 20 billion LY in all directions.

6. Find the top pointer spaces numbered from 10^{13} k to 10^{24} k. Write each distance in the correct number of LY.

a. When we look into the night sky we are looking back in time. Explain, using an example.

b. What is the longest distance you can imagine? Does the billion dot STACK of kilometer tokens help?

trillion K, 10^{13} K = 1 LY, 10^{14} K = 10 LY, 10^{15} K = ... *WOW!*

Copyright © 1994 by TOPS Learning Systems, Canby OR 97013. Reproduction limited to personal classroom use.

Objective

To model the Milky Way Galaxy and understand its orientation in our night sky. To appreciate the vastness of intergalactic space.

Lesson Notes

1. Cotton is fun stuff. Your class will almost certainly use too much. Dole it out, if necessary, 1 pinch to cover the whole circle, another pinch to build up the galactic center.

The Milky Way, in profile, looks rather like 2 fried eggs joined back to back. This paper and cotton model shows only one of these fried eggs. Its haze of cotton suggests billions of stars reaching above the galactic plane.

2a. At a distance of 1,600 LY, Deneb (in the constellation Cygnus) is the only star on your Sky Sphere identified by name that lies outside this arbitrary 1,000 LY limit. Other distant stars not named on the Sky Sphere are the 3 belt stars in Orion (1,500 LY), Orion's foot opposite Rigel (2,100 LY), the easternmost star in Scorpius' tail (3,400 LY) and a few others. Excluding these rare supergiants that shine tens of thousands of times brighter than our sun, all the individual stars we see in the heavens without the aid of a telescope lie inside this "tiny" circle (a sphere when extended into 3 dimensions).

4a. Light from Andromeda is the oldest light that you can see with the naked eye. On a very clear dark night, look for this ancient light above the constellation Andromeda, marked as M 31 on your Sky Sphere. If conditions are right, you'll see its galactic core as a faint hazy patch of light. This light zips into your eye at the usual 300,000 k/sec, but the distance through which it traveled is so incredibly long it took 2.2 million years to arrive!

Answers

√ Kilometer Bar:

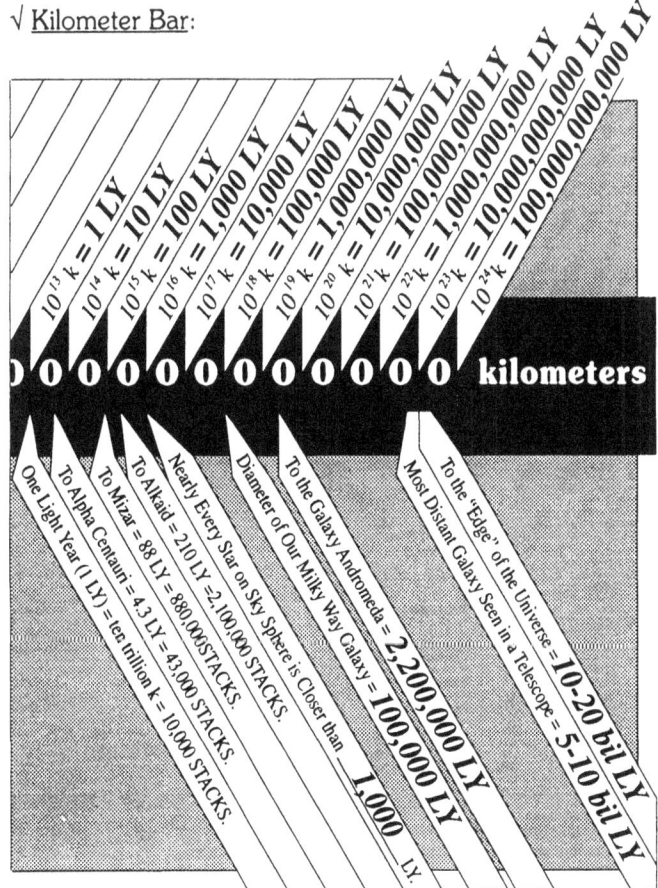

2b. Dubhe lies within the pinhole; it is 105 LY from the sun at the center. Alkaid, at 210 LY, lies a little outside this pinhole. (If this pinhole were enlarged to the scale of your Dipper Box, it would forms a circle around the sun at the view point with a radius of about 1 foot.

3a. Yes. Looking *through* the plane of the galaxy you would expect to see many more stars than looking *out* of it. (You see many more trees looking through a forest than looking up toward the sky.)

3b. The Milky Way, including its galactic center, appear as a grey "fog" on the Sky Sphere. (This edgewise view of the galaxy looks irregular because enormous clouds of dust and gas absorb much of the starlight.)

3c. From our viewpoint inside the Milky Way, we see the plane of the galaxy surrounding us on all sides like a ring. We see only half this ring at a time because the earth blocks our view of the other half.

4b. The Galaxy Ruler has a scale length of 100,000 LY. It fits 22 times into the 2.2 million LY distance between the Milky Way and Andromeda:

2,200,000 LY/100,000 LY = 22 rulers

4c. Separate the Milky Way Disk from the paper plate representing Andromeda by 22 ruler lengths (almost 4 meters).

6a. Light takes time to travel from one place to another. Looking into the night sky across vast reaches of space is a look into the past. The light we now see coming from Alkaid, for example, originally left that star 210 years ago. It took that long to reach Earth. If this star were to blow up *today*, it would take over 2 centuries before our great, great, great, great, great, great grandchildren could witness that event.

6b. Accept all reasoned answers. Using STACKS of newspaper, it is possible to travel huge distances in the mind. For estimating purposes, these rough dimensions might be useful:

1 Billion Travel Tokens

1 STACK =
1,000 layers of newsprint =
1 billion dots (travel tokens)

l STACK ≈ 1 foot x 2 feet x 2.5 feet

Capacity of Classroom = ?

Capacity of RR Boxcar = 6,000 cu feet

Length of RR Boxcar = 55 feet

✓ Milky Way Disk: Does extra cotton fluff up at the galactic center? Does a pinhole mark the sun's position?

✓ Sky Wheel (activity 16): Students should be stargazing at home, adding new stamps to their Sky Wheel as they discover new constellations.

✓ Planet among background stars (activity 19): Advanced students should also be documenting the movement of at least 1 planet by sketching its changing position among the background stars.

Encourage interested students to extend assignments like these into long term science projects. With the sophisticated astronomy tools they now have in hand, the sky is the limit.

Materials

☐ The Milky Way Disk and Galaxy Ruler cutouts.
☐ Scissors and cotton.
☐ Clear tape and a pin.
☐ The Dipper Box and Kilometer Bar.
☐ A paper plate.
☐ The billion dot STACK of newspaper.

SUPPLEMENTARY CUTOUTS

LANDMARK MAPS
ACTIVITY 1

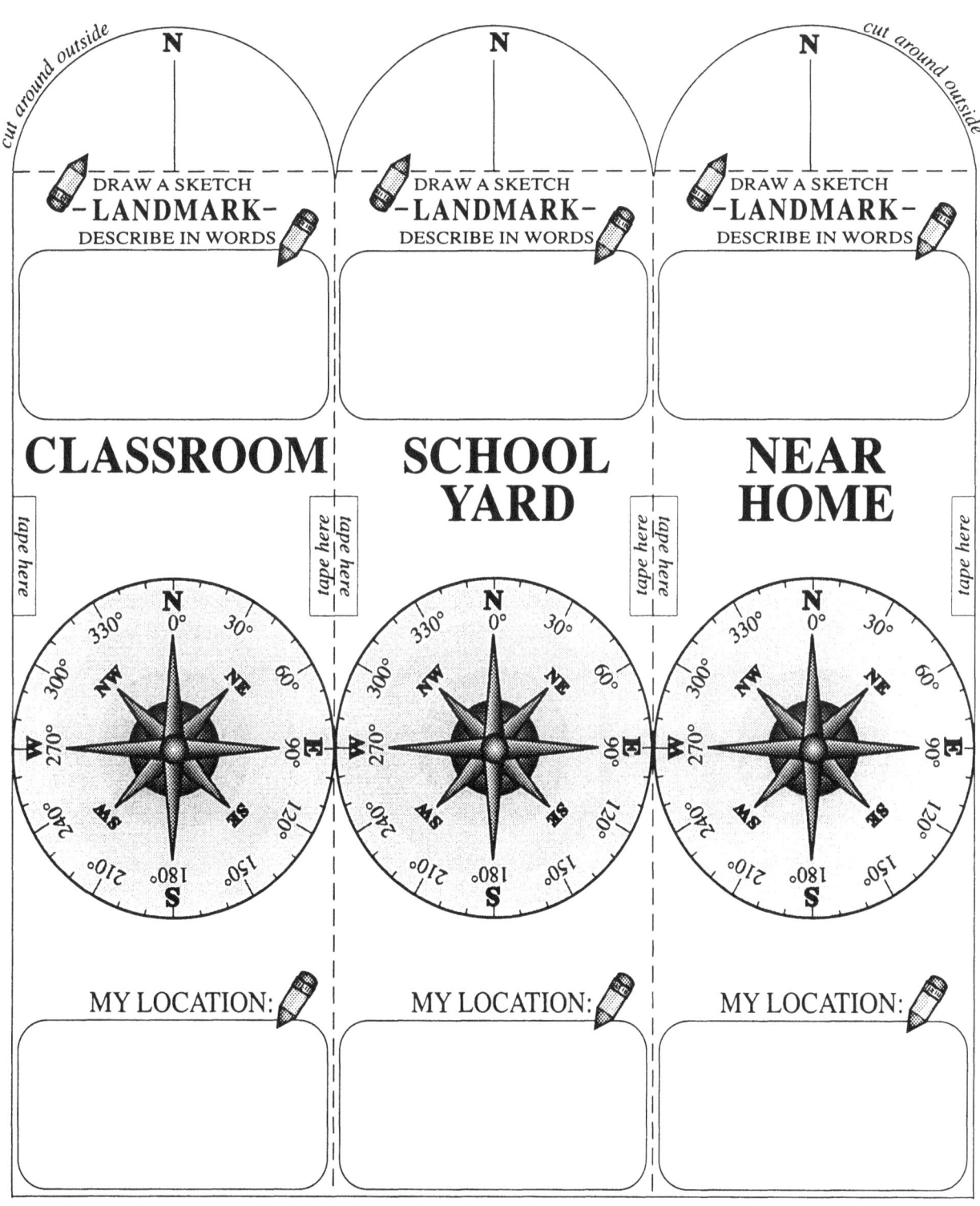

EARTH CIRCLE
ACTIVITY 2

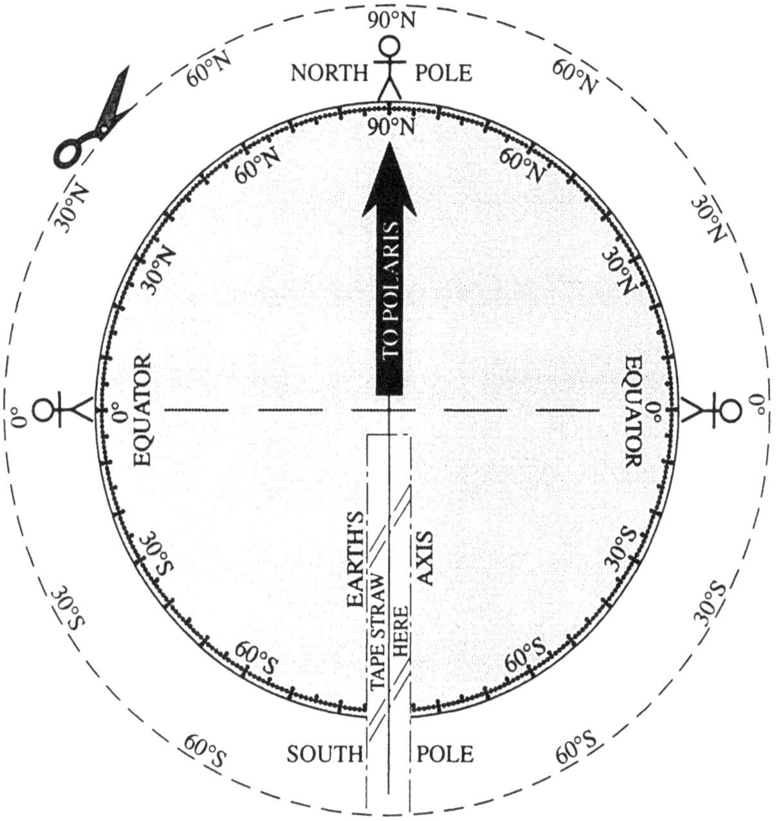

ROUND MAP
ACTIVITY 6

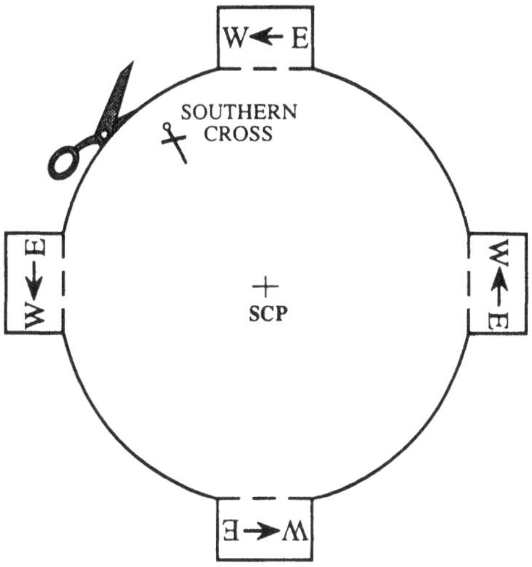

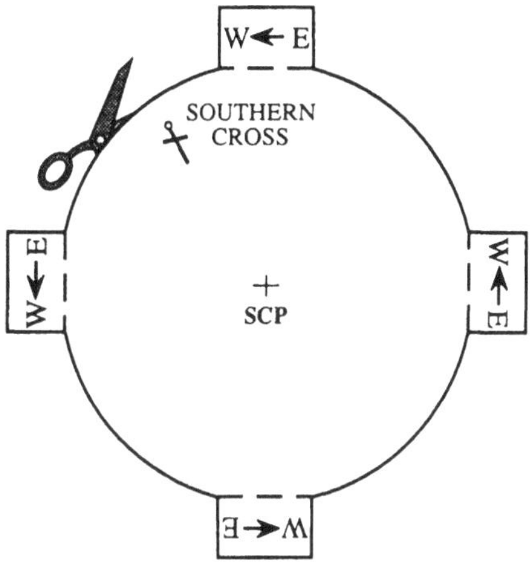

SHADOW SCREEN
ACTIVITY 4

SUN ARROW
ACTIVITY 8

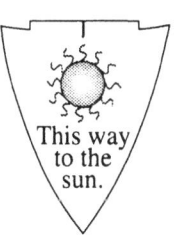

Copyright © 1994 by TOPS Learning Systems, Canby OR 97013. Reproduction limited to personal classroom use.

CONCEPT LIST Activity 2

1. My zenith is always straight overhead. My home stick figure on top of the Earth Circle sees the same stars at its zenith that I do at my zenith.

2. The zeniths of all four stick figures are directed outward from the earth's center, like spokes in a wheel.

3. My home figure's outstretched arms point N and S.

4. If the home figure travels N, it eventually reaches the north pole. If it travels S, it eventually reaches the equator.

5. My outstretched arms trace my home figure's *horizon* as I turn in a circle. I share the same horizon with my home figure on top of the Earth Circle.

6. The arrow labeled "To Polaris" on the Earth Circle points into the sky above the N horizon of my home figure. This is where my home figure sees Polaris, a star in the night sky.

7. Polaris is at the zenith of the north pole figure, and at the N horizon of both equator figures.

8. The long straw rotates east and west through my home figure's southern sky. This traces out its *celestial equator*.

9. In March and September the sun appears to move along my *celestial equator*. During these times, it rises east of my compass rose, culminates over my southern horizon, and sets west of my compass rose.

10. The celestial equator circles the horizon of the north pole figure; it crosses the zeniths of the equator figures.

11. When you fly around the earth's equator, the celestial equator is always straight over your head.

12. The numbers under my home figure's feet (earth latitudes) always equal the numbers over its head (sky declinations). This is true wherever it walks.

CONCEPT LIST Activity 5

1. Tilt the jar so the "pin person" stands straight up on "top" of the earth, surrounded by the stars and sun. This models how I'm standing on "top" of the real world.

2. Turn the clay "sun" to high noon straight over the pin person. This shows that the sun is *not* straight over my head; it is to my south.

3. Earth view: I seem to stand still while the sun and stars move *westward* across my sky.

4. Space view: The earth rotates *eastward* while the sun and stars stand still.

5. You can model how the sun and stars move by turning the jar westward or turning the lid eastward. Either way, the pin person "sees" the same motion.

6. The clay sun appears to move full circle through the fixed background stars once a year. Tiny "suns" mark its position on the *ecliptic circle* at the beginning of each month.

7. The *celestial equator* is located directly above the earth's equator. It is divided into 24 star hours.

8. The sun appears farthest north of the celestial equator about June 21st (summer solstice). It appears farthest south about December 21st (winter solstice).

9. I seem to stand still while the sun and stars move in circles around the North Celestial Pole (NCP). Polaris, over my north horizon, is the only star that seems not to move.

10. The Big Dipper appears to circle counterclockwise in my northern sky. This circle extends from overhead to the horizon.

11. Set your clay "sun" over the fall equinox position at 12h. At that time of year Scorpius culminates near sunset; Pegasus culminates near midnight; Orion culminates near sunrise; Leo culminates near noon.

12. Set your clay sun over the spring equinox position at 0h. At that time of year, Orion culminates near sunset; Leo culminates near midnight; Scorpius culminates near sunrise; Pegasus culminates near noon.

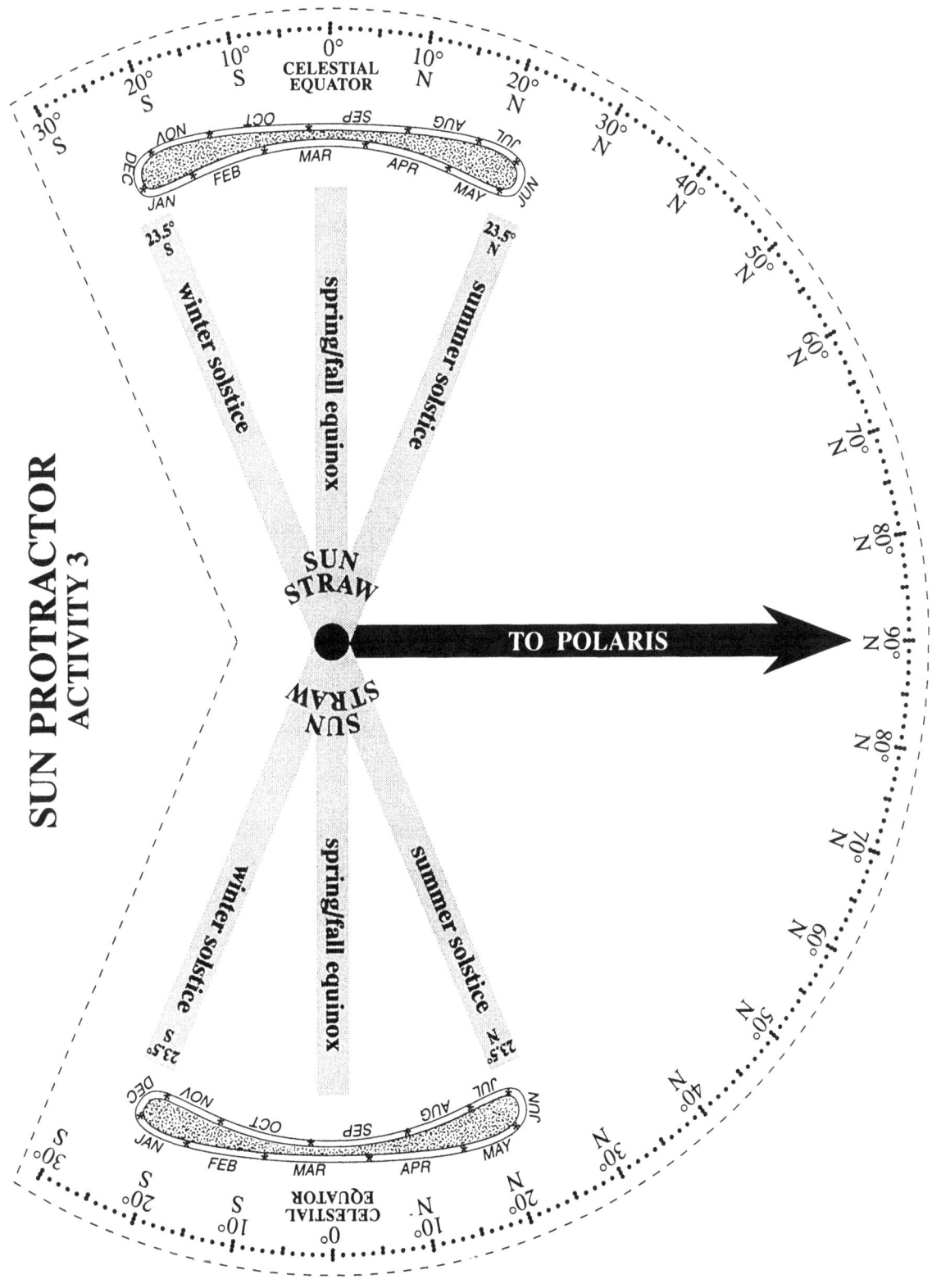

LONG MAPS — ACTIVITY 5

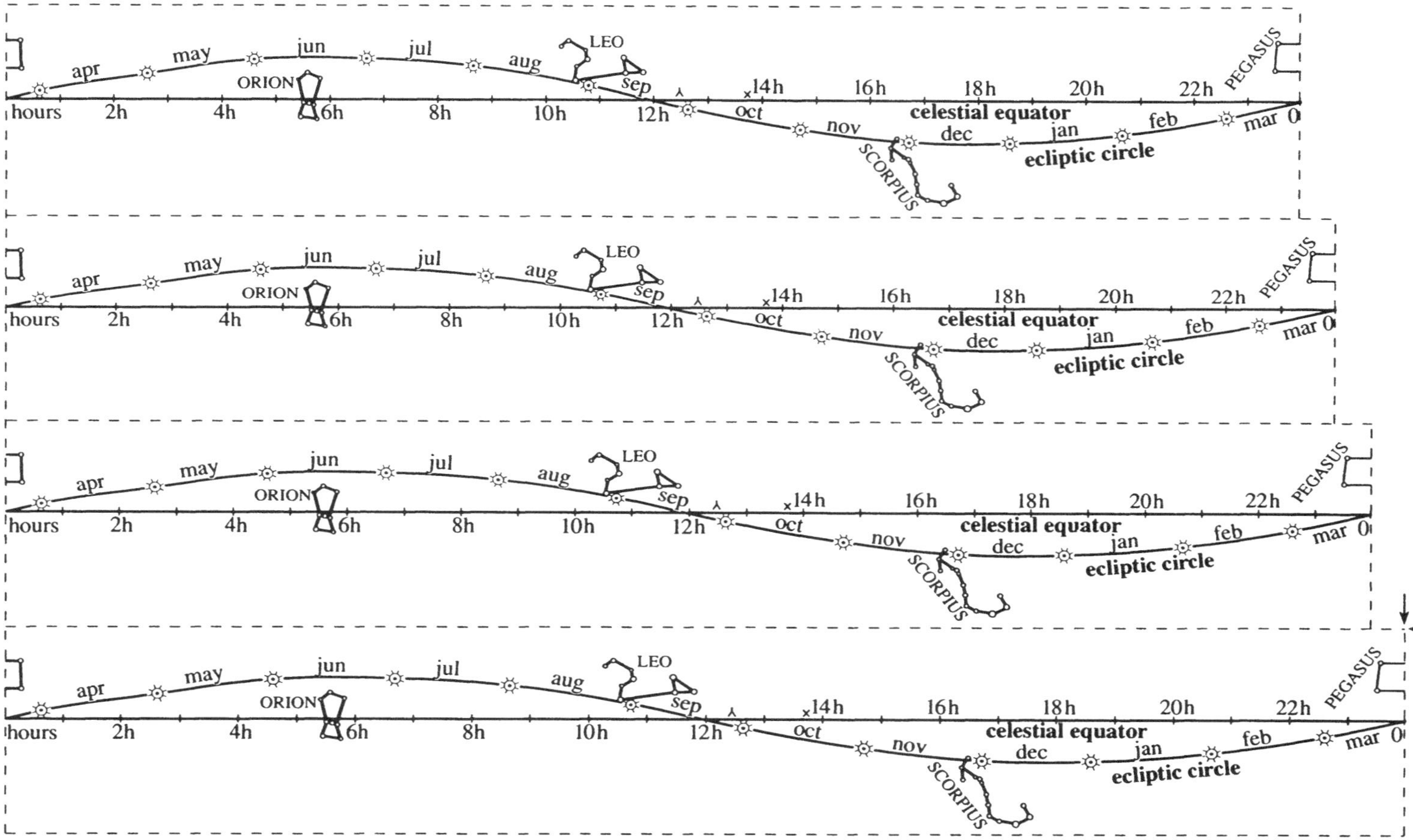

SHORT MAP — Activity 5
Cut it out INSIDE the dashed line.

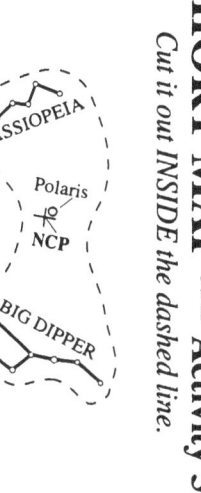

COMPASS CIRCLE
Activity 5
Cut out with a paper punch.

Cut on dashed lines.

Copyright © 1994 by TOPS Learning Systems, Canby OR 97013. Reproduction limited to personal classroom use.

CONCEPT TABLE
Activity 6

At the EQUATOR:	At MY NORTH LATITUDE:	At the NORTH POLE:
1a. Polaris appears fixed *on* my N horizon.	**1b.** Polaris appears fixed *above* my N horizon.	**1c.** Polaris appears fixed at my zenith.
2a. Cassiopeia rises in the NE and sets in the NW.	**2b.** Cassiopeia dips low to my N horizon and rises overhead.	**2c.** Cassiopeia circles around my zenith.
3a. Orion rises in the east, culminates at my zenith, and sets in the west.	**3b.** Orion rises in the east, culminates to my south, and sets in the west.	**3c.** Orion circles parallel to my horizon.
4a. The Southern Cross rises in the SE and sets in the SW.	**4b.** The Southern Cross almost rises at my S horizon.	**4c.** The Southern Cross remains far below my horizon.
5a. All of the stars rise above my horizon.	**5b.** Most of the stars rise above my horizon.	**5c.** Half of the stars always stay above my horizon.
6a. In June the sun culminates north of my zenith. In December it culminates south.	**6b.** In June the sun culminates high in the south. In December it culminates low in the south.	**6c.** In June the sun never sets. In December it never rises.

CONCEPT LIST
Activity 14

1. Your Sky Sphere maps the same starry sky as your Star Jar.

2. The celestial equator on your Sky Sphere is the same as the celestial equator on your Star Jar.

3. The ecliptic circle on your Sky Sphere is the same as the ecliptic circle on your Star Jar.

4. Find your window-tracing of Orion near 5h on the celestial equator. To see this constellation *inside* your Sky Sphere, look through the 15h window.

5. Find your window-tracing of Pegasus near 23h. To see this constellation *inside* your Sky Sphere, look through either the 7h window or the 15h window.

6. Locate the Big Dipper north of Leo inside your Sky Sphere. Merak and Dubhe (2 stars in the Dipper's cup) point to Polaris near the North Celestial Pole (NCP).

7. Find the handle of the Big Dipper. Follow its arc to Arcturus (in Bootes), then continue along this curve to Spica (in Virgo).

8. Arcturus is N of the celestial equator in Bootes. Spica is S of the celestial equator in Virgo. These stars point to Crux (also called the Southern Cross) far to the south.

9. The belt of Orion points north of the celestial equator toward Aldebaran (in Taurus) and south toward Sirius (in Canis Major).

10. Locate the Guardians of the Pole on your Polar Graph. Find these same 2 stars in Ursa Minor (also called the Little Dipper) in your Sky Sphere.

11. Your Polar Graph maps part of the same sky as your Sky Sphere.

12. The sun's position is too far south to be plotted on the Polar Graph. The Sun Arrow can only point in its direction.

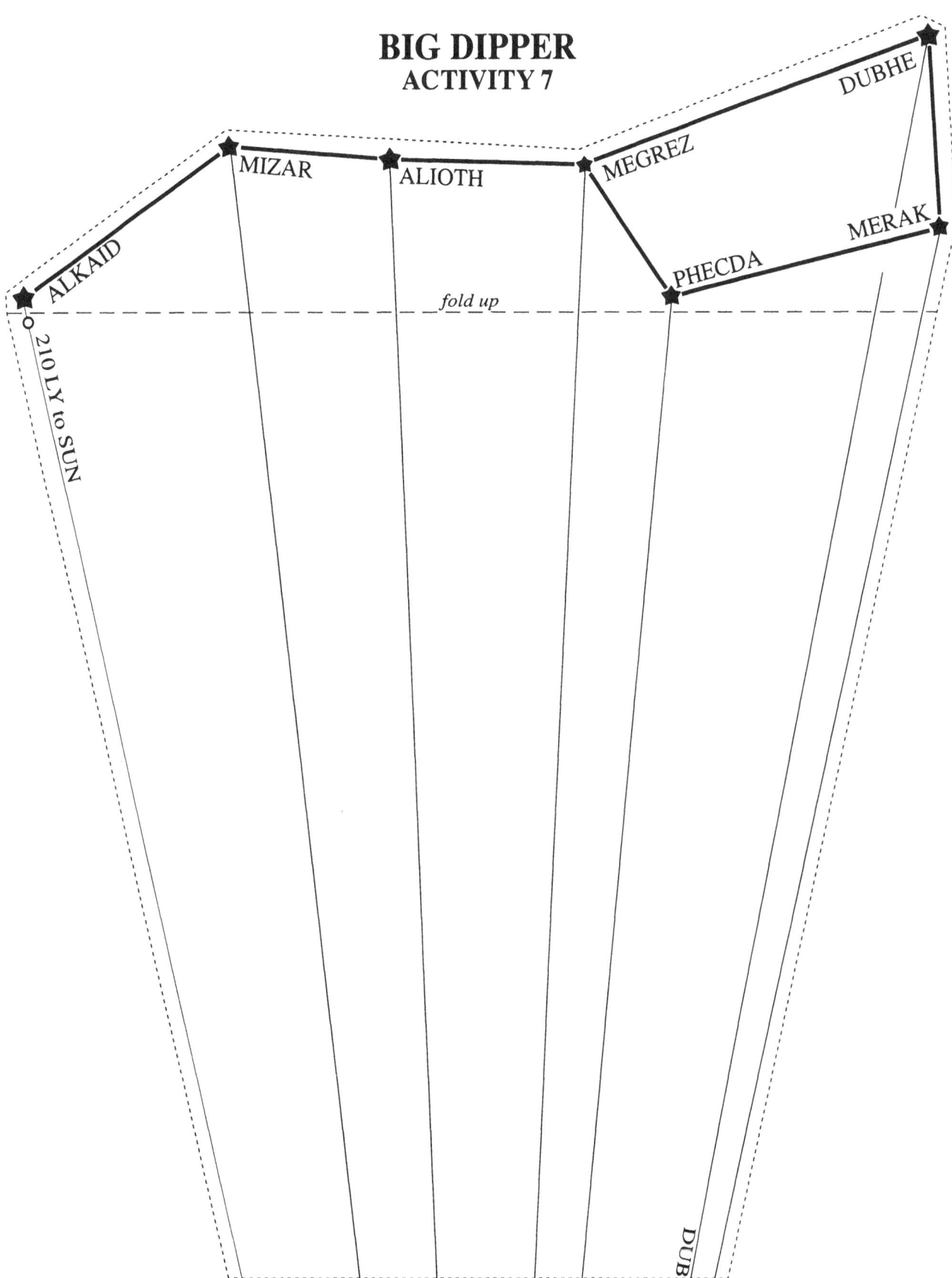

VIEW POINT
ACTIVITY 7

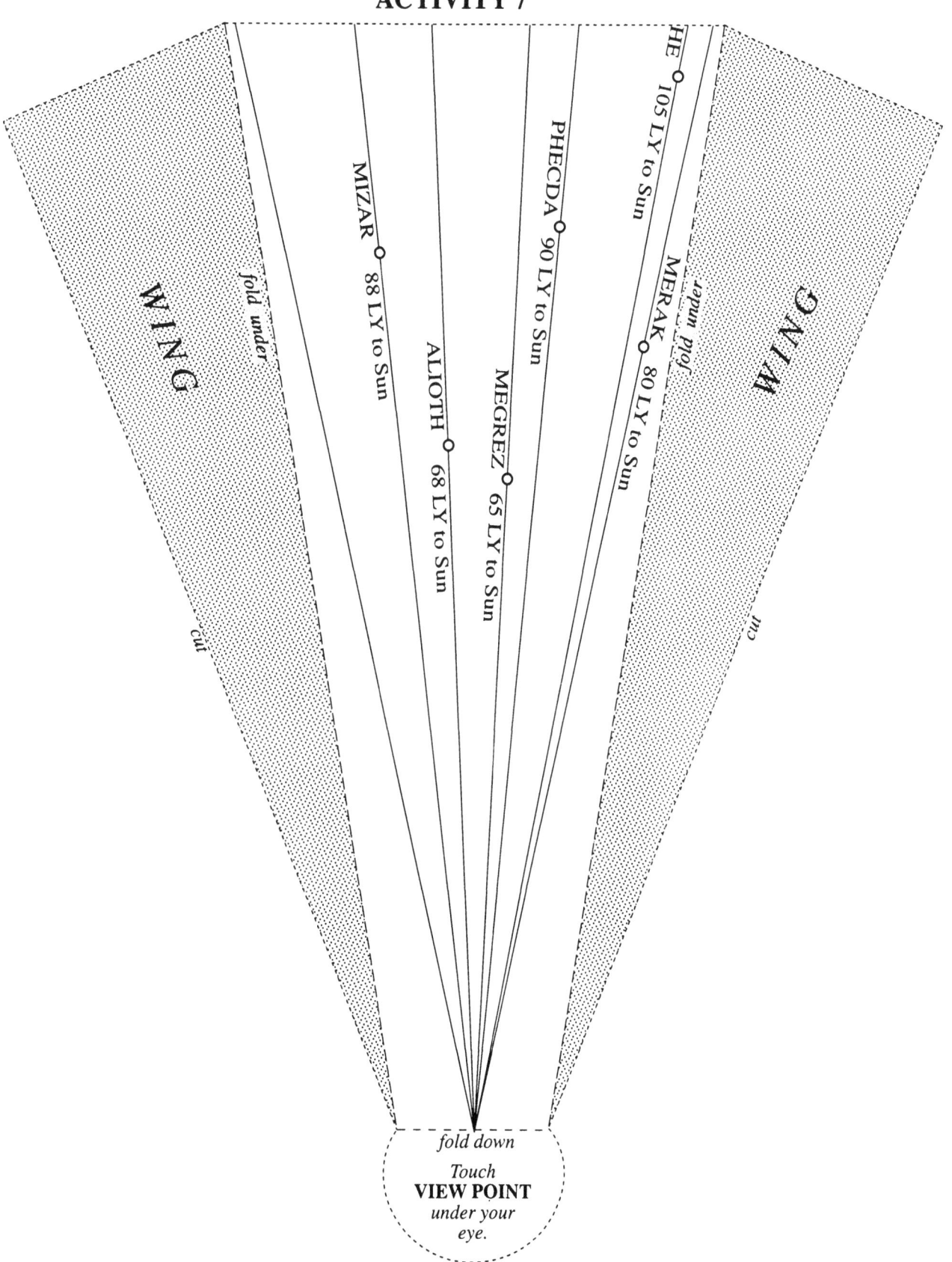

Copyright © 1994 by TOPS Learning Systems, Canby OR 97013. Reproduction limited to personal classroom use.

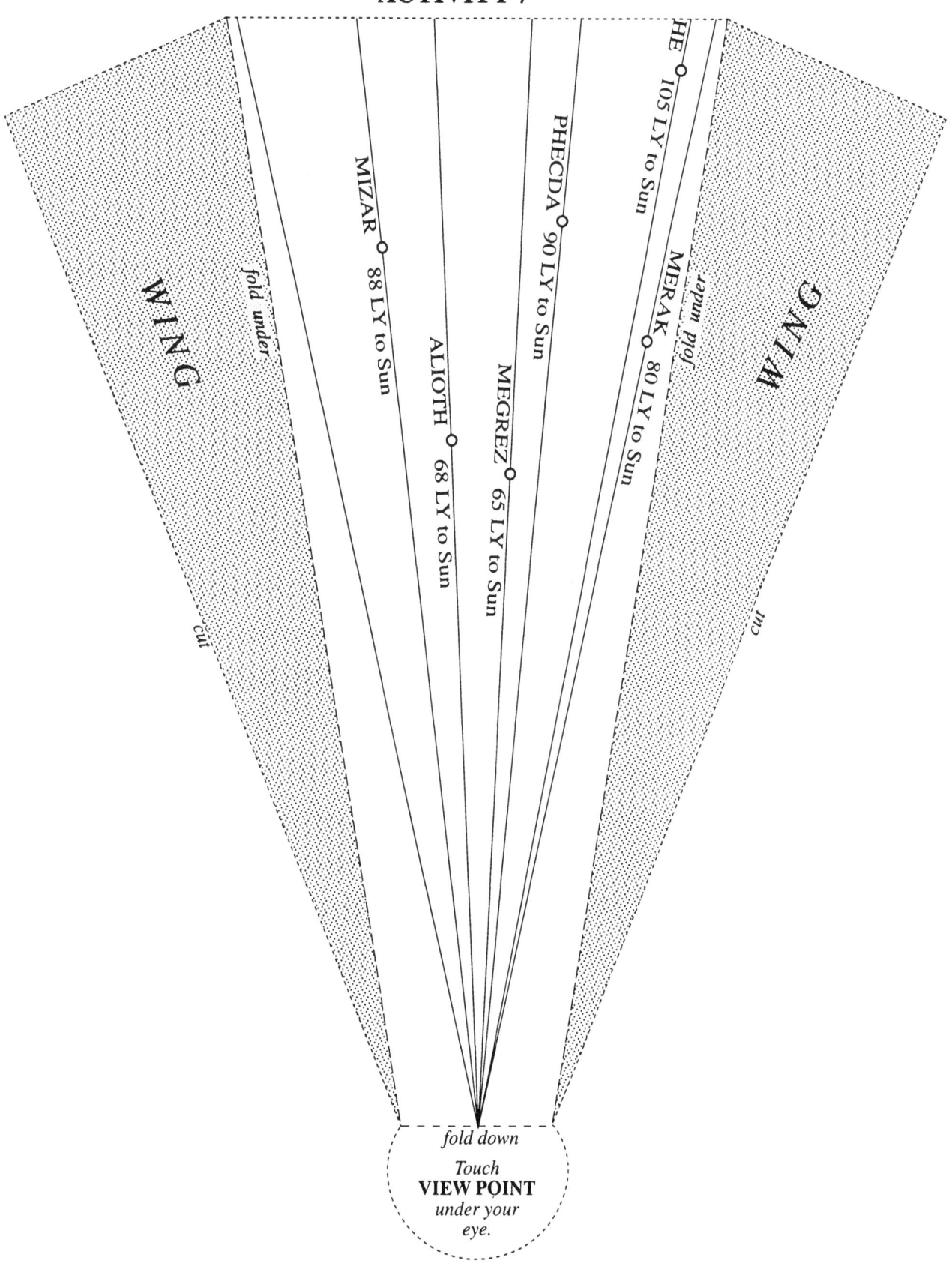

VIEWING DISTANCE FOR ACTUAL SIZE

POLAR GRAPH
ACTIVITY 8

(Polar graph with hour markings 0h–23h around the perimeter and declination circles from 40° to NCP=90°)

Copyright © 1994
by TOPS Learning Systems, Canby OR 97013.
Reproduction limited to personal classroom use.

CASSIOPEIA
Known as the queen.

ORDER of discovery (1, 2 or 3?)	DATE (month/day)
	HOUR (with am/pm)

ACTIVITY 9:
(Fill in these night sky observations as weather permits.)

The Big Dipper (URSA MAJOR)
This is part of a larger constellation called Ursa Major (the Big Bear).

ORDER of discovery (1, 2 or 3?)	DATE (month/day)
	HOUR (with am/pm)

- Estimate the apparent separation between Dubhe and Polaris: _____
- Find a dim companion to one of the Dipper stars. Draw it on your graph in the correct position and label it Alcor.

Guardians / Pole Star (URSA MINOR)
These are part of the constellation Ursa Minor (the Little Bear), also called the Little Dipper.

ORDER of discovery (1, 2 or 3?)	DATE (month/day)
	HOUR (with am/pm)

STAR RULER — ACTIVITY 12

ANGLE FINDER — ACTIVITY 9

cut ... *fold up*
- 5°
- 10°
- 20°

5°
10°
20°

fold down / *flap* / *cut*

VIEW POINT *fold down* / *cut*

STAR RULER

Light Years (LY)	Average Spacing (1 star per cube)	Average Spacing (1 star per cube)	Degrees
1, 3, 5	1		1°
10	2	1	2°
			3°
20	3	2	4°
			5°
	4	3	6°
30			7°
	5	4	8°
40			9°
	6	5	10°
			11°
50	7	6	12°
			13°
60	8	7	14°
			15°
	9	8	16°
70			17°
	10	9	18°
80			19°
	11	10	20°
			21°
90	12	11	22°
			23°
100	13	12	24°
			25°
	14	13	26°
110			27°
	15	14	28°
120			29°
	16	15	30°
			31°
	17	16	32°
130	18	17, 18	33°

Copyright © 1994 by TOPS Learning Systems, Canby OR 97013. Reproduction limited to personal classroom use.

LOTS-O-DOTS — ACTIVITY 10

Copyright © 1994 by TOPS Learning Systems, Canby OR 97013. Reproduction limited to personal classroom use.

KILOMETER BAR — ACTIVITY 11

Top Pointer Spaces:

Bottom Pointer Spaces:

one k

10^{13} k
one trillion k
10^{14} k

10^{24} k

1 0 0 0 0 0 0 0 0 0 0 0 0 0 0 0 0 0 0 0 0 0 0 0 kilometers

- 1 kilometer = 2.5 laps =
- 10 kilometers =
- 100 kilometers =
- 1,000 kilometers =
- One Earth Diameter (1 ED) =
- Diameter of Jupiter =
- One Light Second (LS) =
- One Astronomical Unit (1 AU) = _____ (to Moon)
- One Light Hour (LH) =
- Diameter of Our Solar System = _____ k = _____ STACK. (to Saturn) (to Sun)
- One Light Year (1 LY) =
- To Alpha Centauri =
- To Mizar = _____ LY = _____ k =
- To Alkaid = _____ LY = _____ STACKS.
- Nearly Every Star on Sky Sphere is Closer than _____ STACKS.
- Diameter of Our Milky Way Galaxy = _____ STACKS.
- To the Galaxy Andromeda = _____ LY.
- Most Distant Galaxy Seen in a Telescope =
- To the "Edge" of the Universe =

Copyright © 1994 by TOPS Learning Systems, Canby OR 97013. Reproduction limited to personal classroom use.

SOLAR SYSTEM SQUARES — ACTIVITY 13

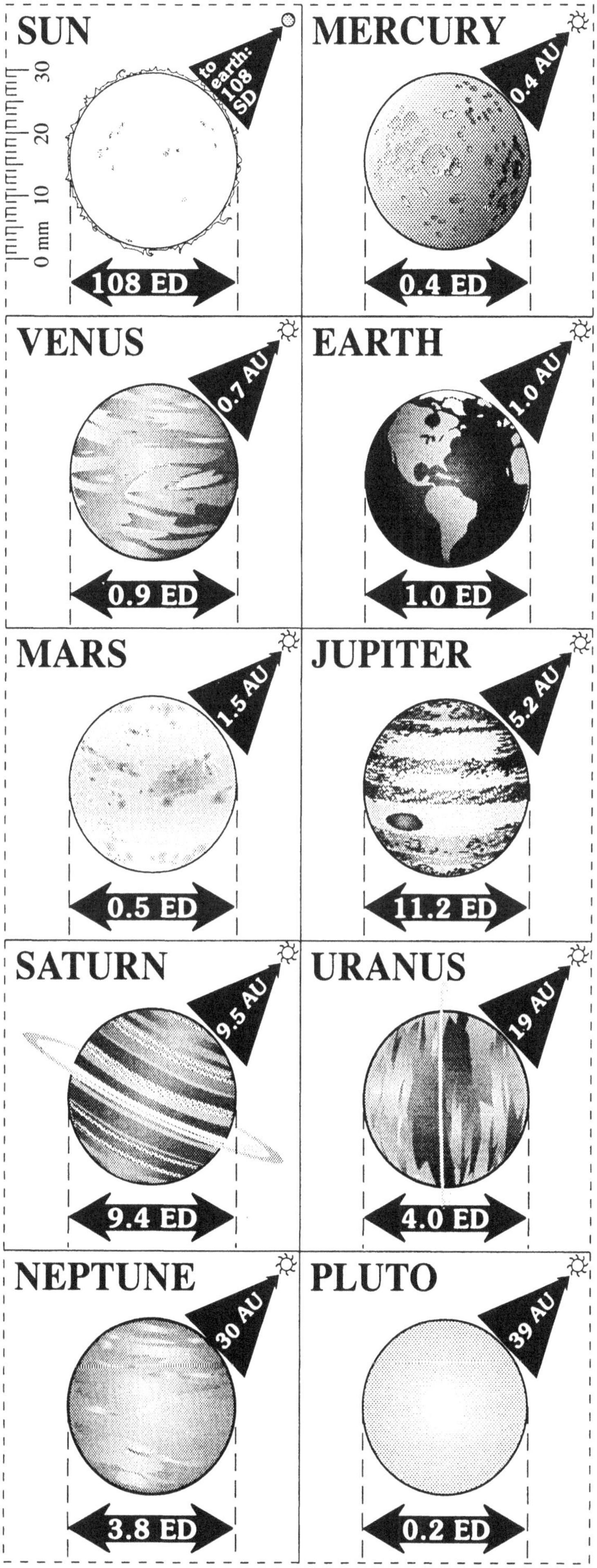

SUN	MERCURY
to earth: 108 SD	0.4 AU
108 ED	0.4 ED

VENUS	EARTH
0.7 AU	1.0 AU
0.9 ED	1.0 ED

MARS	JUPITER
1.5 AU	5.2 AU
0.5 ED	11.2 ED

SATURN	URANUS
9.5 AU	1.9 AU
9.4 ED	4.0 ED

NEPTUNE	PLUTO
30 AU	39 AU
3.8 ED	0.2 ED

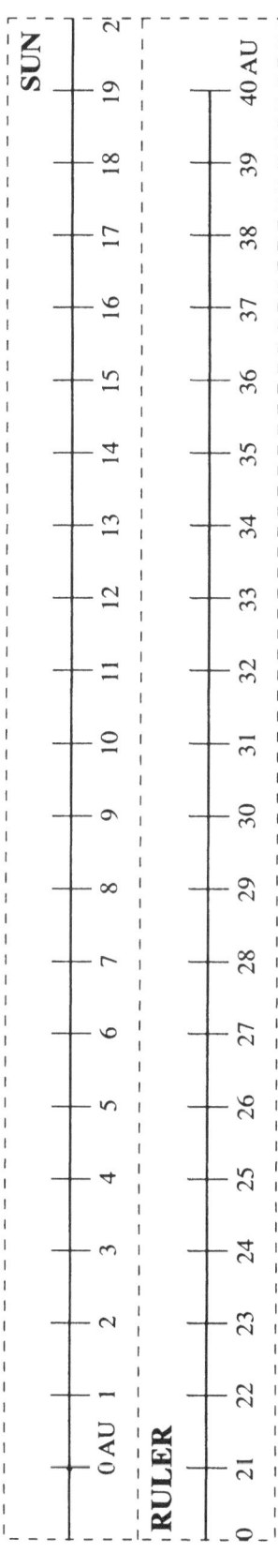

SUN RULER
ACTIVITY 13

Copyright © 1994
TOPS Learning Systems, Canby OR 97013.
Reproduction limited to personal classroom use.

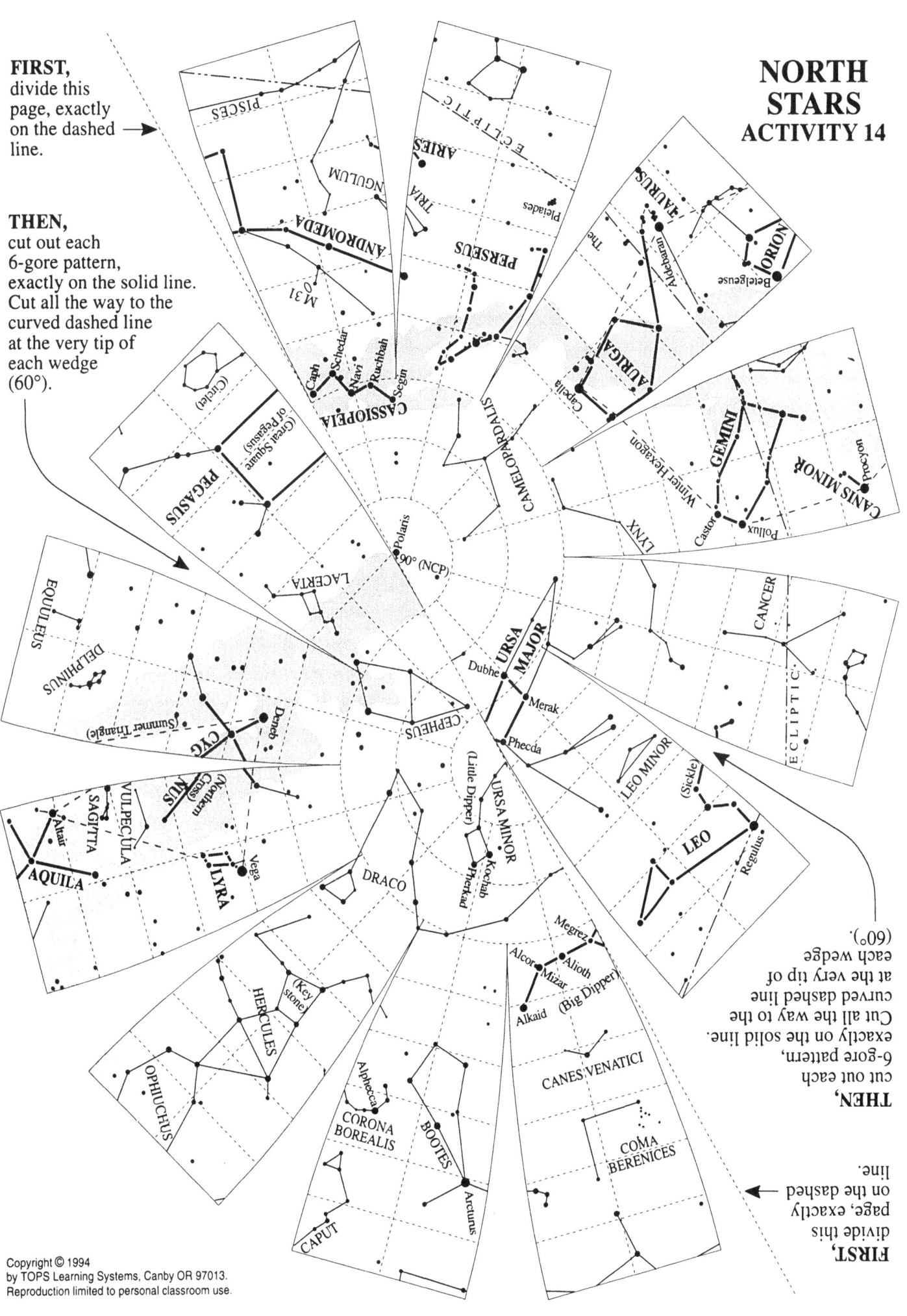

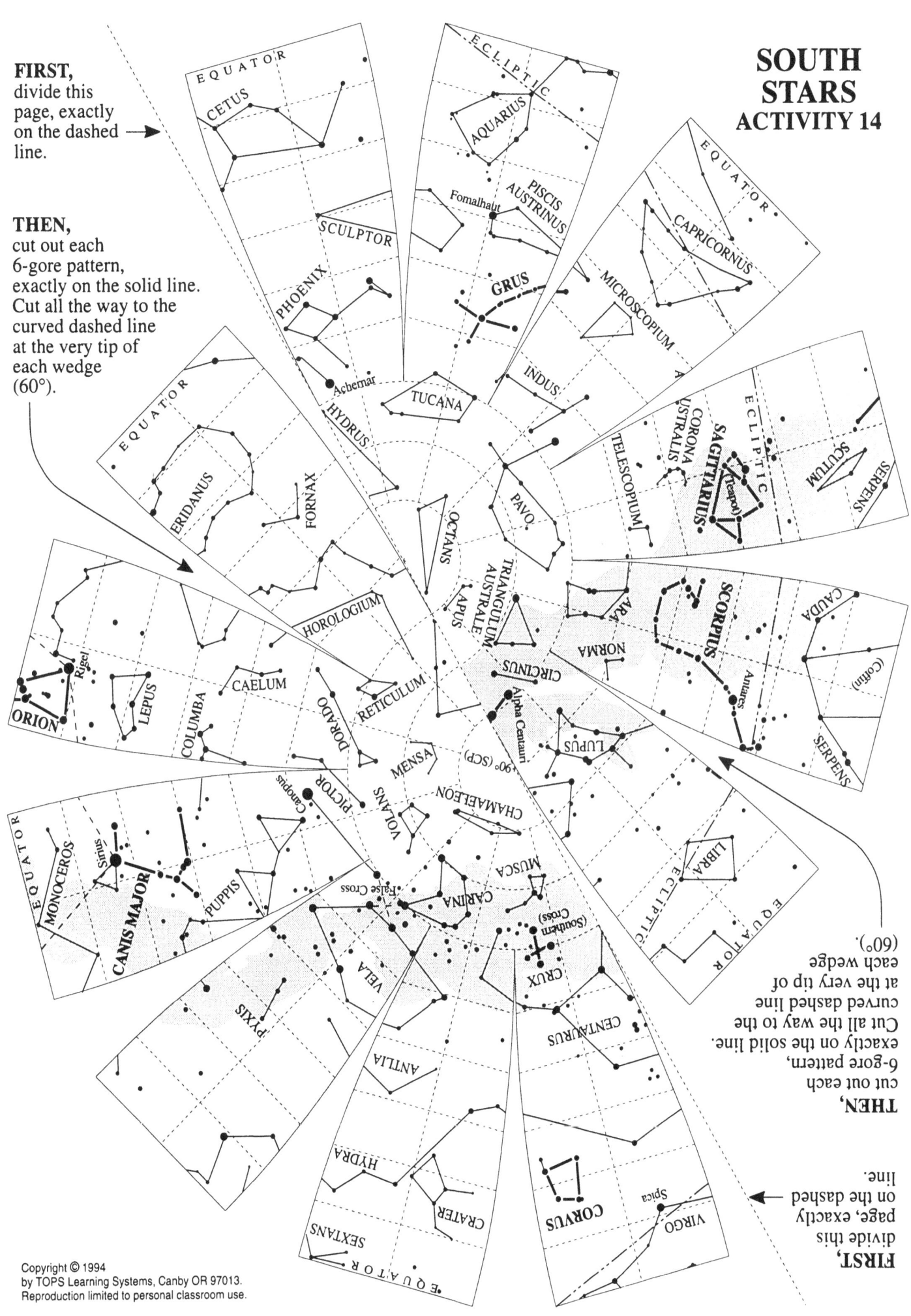

ZODIAC RING
ACTIVITY 15

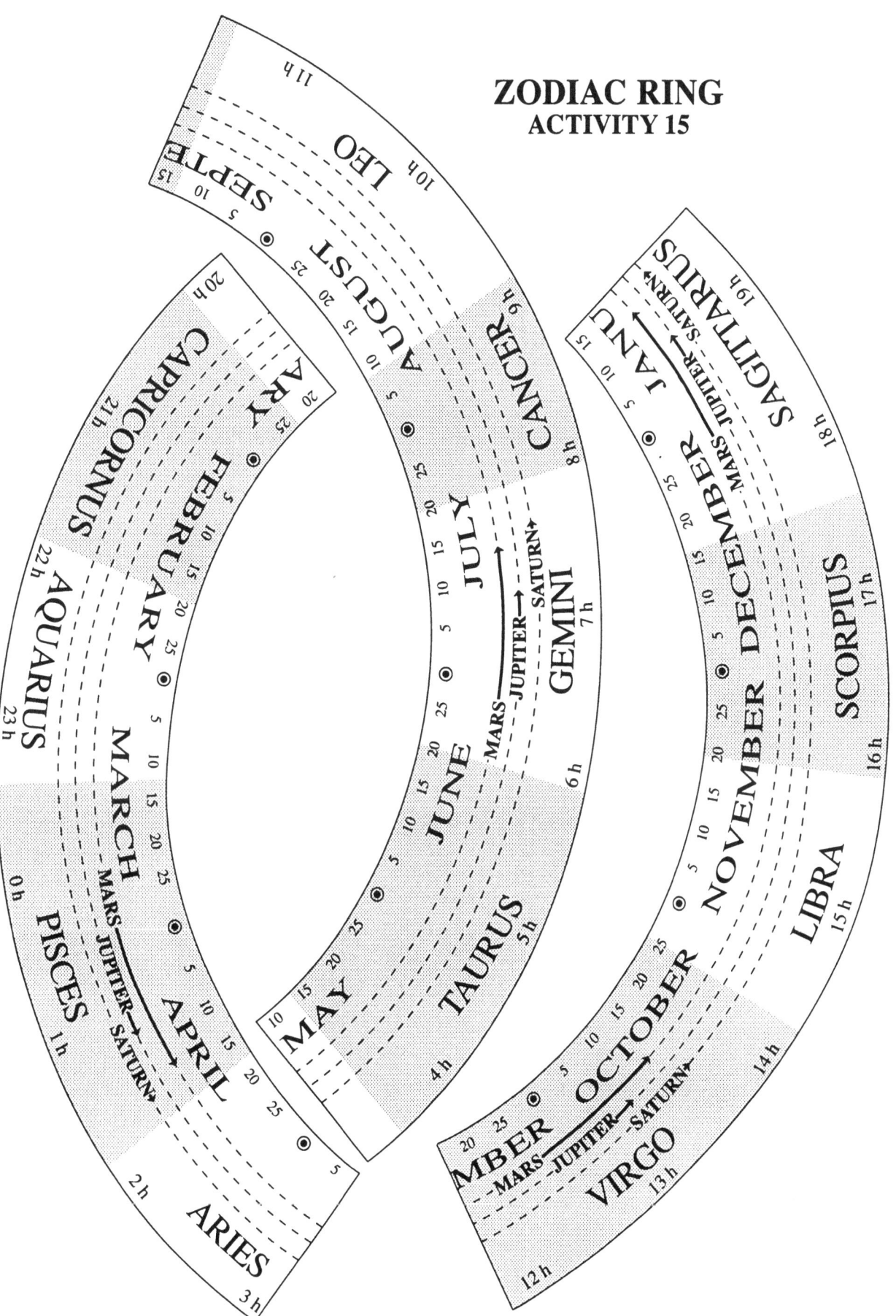

EARTH RULER
ACTIVITY 17

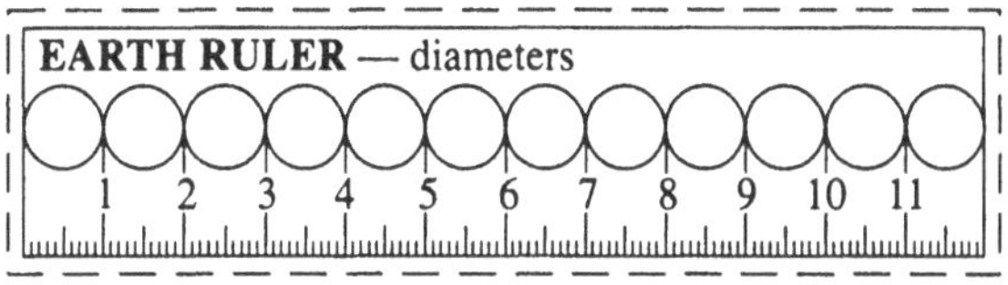

SKY TABS — ACTIVITY 15

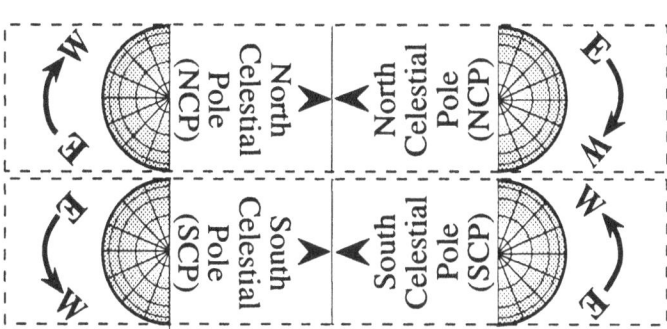

PLANET FINDER
ACTIVITY 19

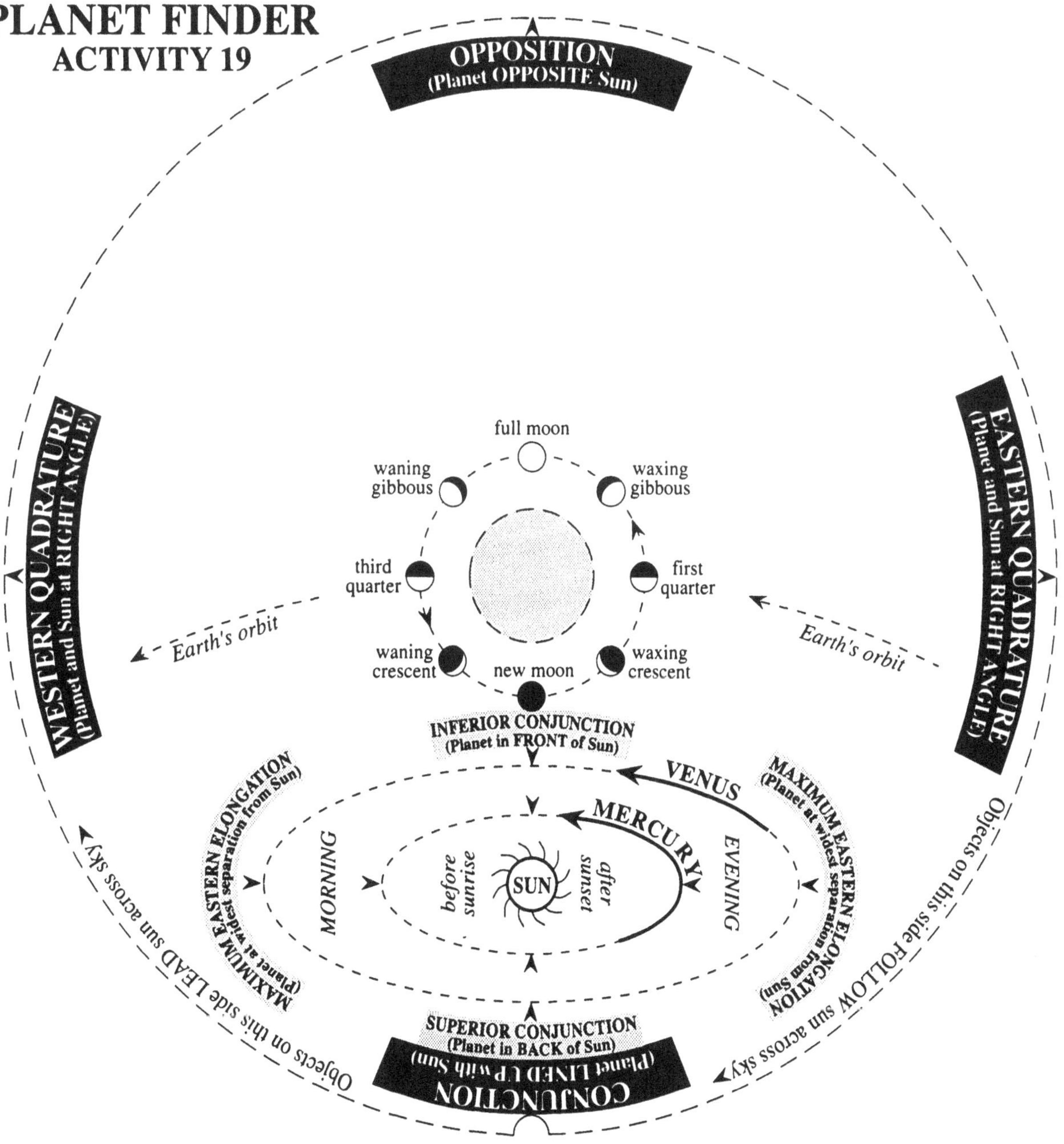

CONCEPT LIST Activity 16

1. Rotate your Sky Sphere so Orion rises due east, crosses your meridian, and sets due west. Meanwhile, Polaris hardly moves at all.

2. As Orion culminates at your meridian, Leo rises to your east and Pegasus sets to your west.

3. Hold the Sky Sphere over your head so you can look *inside* the sphere to see Orion crossing your meridian.

4. Look *inside* your sky sphere to see Orion, Auriga and Lepus all cross your meridian at the same time.

5. Perseus, Auriga and Gemini move across my meridian in that order.

6. Pegasus, Andromeda and Perseus move across my meridian in that order.

7. Scorpius, Sagittarius and Capricornus move across my meridian in that order. I see this looking both inside and outside the Sky Sphere.

8. As I tilt the Sky Sphere toward Polaris and turn it from east to west, all stars in the yellow NCP circle go round and round but never set.

9. As I tilt the Sky Sphere toward Polaris and turn it from east to west, all stars in the yellow SCP circle go round and round but never rise.

10. Cassiopeia always circles *above* your horizon; the Southern Cross always circles *below* your horizon; Orion circles equally above and below your horizon.

11. In June, the sun reaches its most northerly summer position as it leaves the constellation Taurus and moves into Gemini. This is a bad time of year to see Orion, but a good time of year to see Scorpius.

12. In March, the sun leaves Aquarius, passing northward across the celestial equator into Pisces. This is a bad time of year to see Pegasus, but a good time of year to see Leo.

CONCEPT LIST Activity 19

1. The sun, moon, planets and stars all appear to turn full circle on a daily basis, with you at the center.

2. A planet at eastern quadrature seems to *follow* the sun in its daily journey across the sky. A planet at western quadrature seems to *lead* the sun.

3. A first quarter moon is at eastern quadrature: it seems to *follow* the sun in its daily journey across the sky. A third quarter moon is at western quadrature: it seems to *lead* the sun.

4. Turn your paper clip "sun" to its midnight position. The tape tags on the ecliptic circle now show where to find the moon and planets <u>at midnight</u>.

5. Turn your paper clip "sun" so it is setting in the west. The tape tags on the ecliptic circle now show where to find the moon and planets <u>at sunset</u>.

6. Turn your paper clip "sun" to its current position in your sky. The tape tags on the ecliptic circle show where to find the moon and planets <u>right now</u>.

7. The word "planet" comes from a Greek word meaning "wanderer." These planets are so named because they appear to move from month to month against a fixed background of zodiac constellations.

8. Mercury takes about 3 months to orbit the sun; Venus takes about 7 months; Mars takes about 22 months.

9. Mercury and Venus always appear close to the sun. They never appear in opposition like Mars, Jupiter and Saturn.

10. During eastern elongation, Venus is commonly called the evening "star." During western elongation it is known as the morning "star."

11. The moon appears to circle westward once a day, while it drifts eastward in a full circle once a month.

12. The sun appears to circle westward once a day, while it drifts eastward in a full circle once a year.

SKY DICTIONARY — Activity 16

Vowels with bars have long sounds: āce, bē, sīde, bōne, ūse.
Unmarked vowels have short sounds: cat, red, sit, top, cup.
The letters "ah" sound like banana.

CONSTELLATIONS

* **ANDROMEDA** an-drom/ e-dah *The daughter* * **ANTLIA** ant/ lē-ah *Air Pump* * **APUS** ā/ pus *Bird of Paradise* * **AQUARIUS** a-kwar/ ē-us *Water Carrier* * **AQUILA** ak/ will-ah *Eagle* * **ARA** ā/ rah *Altar* * **ARIES** air/ ēz *Ram* * **AURIGA** o-rī/ gah *Charioteer* * **BOOTES** bō-ō/ tēz *Herdsman* * **CAELUM** sē/ lum *Chisel* * **CAMELOPARDALIS** ka-mel/ o-par/ da-lis *Giraffe* * **CANCER** kan/ ser *Crab* * CANES VENATICI kā/ nēz vē-nat/ i-sī *Hunting Dogs* * **CANIS MAJOR** kā/ nis mā/ jer *Big Dog* * **CANIS MINOR** kā/ nis mī/ ner *Little Dog* * **CAPRICORNUS** kap/ ri-kor/ nus *Goat* * **CARINA** kah-rī/ nah *Ship's Keel* * **CASSIOPEIA** kas/ ē-o-pē/ yah *The Queen* * **CENTAURUS** sen-tō/ rus *Centaur* * **CEPHEUS** sē/ fus *The King* * **CETUS** sē/ tus *Whale* * **CHAMAELEON** ka-mē/ lē-un *Chameleon* * **CIRCINUS** sur/ si-nus *Compasses* * **COLUMBA** ko-lum/ bah *Dove* * **COMA BERENICES** kō/ mah ber/ e-nī/ sēz *Berenice's Hair* * **CORONA AUSTRALIS** kō-rō/ nah os-trā/ lis *Southern Crown* * **CORONA BOREALIS** kō-rō/ nah bō/ rē-a/ lis *Northern Crown* * **CORVUS** kor/ vus *Crow* * **CRATER** krā/ ter *Cup* * **CRUX** kruks *Southern Cross* * **CYGNUS** sig/ nus *Swan* * **DELPHINUS** del-fī/ nus *Dolphin* * **DORADO** do-rā/ dō *Swordfish* * **DRACO** drā/ kō *Dragon* * **EQUULEUS** ē-kwoo/ lē-us *Little Horse* * **ERIDANUS** ē-rid/ ah-nus *The River* * **FORNAX** for/ naks *Furnace* * **GEMINI** jem/ i-nī *Twins* * **GRUS** grus *Crane* * **HERCULES** hur/ kū/ lēz *The Strong Man* * **HOROLOGIUM** hor/ ō-lō/ jē-um *Clock* * **HYDRA** hī/ drah *Sea Serpent* * **HYDRUS** hī/ drus *Water Snake* * **INDUS** in/ dus *Indian* * **LACERTA** lah-sur/ tah *Lizard* * **LEO** lē/ ō *Lion* * **LEO MINOR** lē/ ō mī/ ner *Little Lion* * **LEPUS** lē/ pus *Hare* * **LIBRA** lī/ -brah *Scales* * **LUPUS** loo/ pus *Wolf* * **LYNX** lingks *Lynx* * **LYRA** lī/ rah *Lyre* * **MENSA** men/ sah *Table Mountain* * **MICROSCOPIUM** mī/ krō-skō/ pē-um *Microscope* * **MONOCEROS** mō-nos/ er-os *Unicorn* * **MUSCA** mus/ kah *Fly* * **NORMA** nor/ mah *The Square* * **OCTANS** ok/ tanz *Octant* * **OPHIUCHUS** of/ ē-ū/ kus *Serpent Holder* * **ORION** ō-rī/ on *The Hunter* * **PAVO** pā/ vō *Peacock* * **PEGASUS** peg/ ah-sus *Winged Horse* * **PERSEUS** pur/ sē-us *The Champion* * **PHOENIX** fē/ niks *The Bird* * **PICTOR** pik/ ter *Easel* * **PISCES** pīs/ ēz *Fishes* * **PISCIS AUSTRINUS** pīs/ is os-trī/ nus *Southern Fish* * **PUPPIS** pup/ is *Ship's Stern* * **PYXIS** pik/ sis *Ship's Compass* * **RECTICULUM** re-tik/ ū-lum *Net* * **SAGITTA** sah-jit/ ah *Arrow* * **SAGITTARIUS** saj/ i-tār/ ē-us *Archer* * **SCORPIUS** skor/ pē-us *Scorpion* * **SCULPTOR** skulp/ ter *Sculptor* * **SCUTUM** skū/ tum *Shield* * **SERPENS CAPUT** sur/ penz kā/ put *Serpent's Head* * **SERPENS CAUDA** sur/ penz kow/ dah *Serpent's Tail* * **SEXTANS** seks/ tanz *Sextant* * **TAURUS** to/ rus *Bull* * **TELESCOPIUM** tel/ e-skō/ pē-um *Telescope* * **TRIANGULUM** trī-ang/ gū-lum *Triangle* * **TRIANGULUM AUSTRALE** tri-ang/ gū-lum os-trā/ lah *Southern Triangle* * **TUCANA** too-kā/ nah *Toucan* * **URSA MAJOR** ur/ sah mā/ jer *Great Bear* * **URSA MINOR** ur/ sah mī/ ner *Little Bear* * **VELA** vē/ lah *Ship's Sail* * **VIRGO** vur/ gō *Virgin* * **VOLANS** vō/ lanz *Flying Fish* * **VULPECULA** vul-pek/ ū-lah *Little Fox* *

STARS

* **Achernar** ā/ ker-nar * **Alcor** al/ kor * **Aldebaran** al-deb/ ah-ran * **Alioth** al/ ē-oth * **Alkaid** al-kād/ * **Alpha Centauri** al/ fah cen-tō/ rī * **Alphecca** al-fek/ ah * **Altair** al-tār/ * **Antares** an-tā/ rēz * **Arcturus** ark-too/ rus * **Betelgeuse** bet/ al-joos * **Canopus** ka-nō/ pus * **Capella** kah-pel/ ah * **Caph** kaff * **Castor** kas/ ter * **Deneb** den/ eb * **Dubhe** doob/ ē * **Fomalhaut** fō/ mal-ot * **Kochab** kō/ kab * **Megrez** Mē/ grez * **Merak** mē/ rak * **Mizar** mī/ zer * **Nave** nah/ vē * **Phecda** fek/ dah * **Pherkad** fer/ kad * **Polaris** pō-lar/ iss * **Pollux** pol/ uks * **Procyon** prō/ sē-on * **Regulus** rā/ gū-lus * **Rigel** rī/ jel * **Ruchbah** rook/ bah * **Schedar** shed/ ar * **Segin** Se/ gin * **Sirius** seer/ ē-us * **Spica** spī/ kah * **Vega** vā/ gah *

SKY WHEEL
ACTIVITY 16

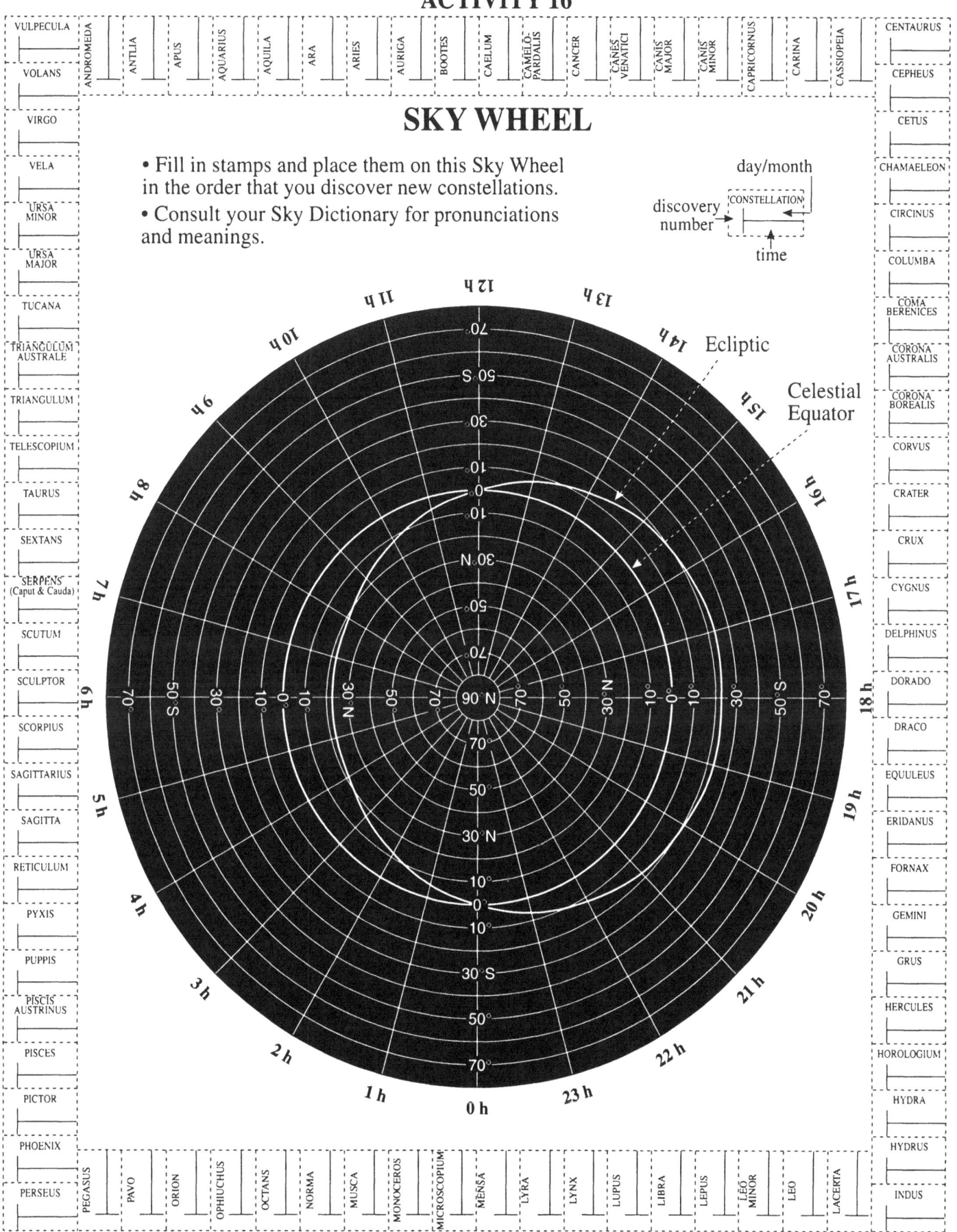

SKY WHEEL

- Fill in stamps and place them on this Sky Wheel in the order that you discover new constellations.
- Consult your Sky Dictionary for pronunciations and meanings.

Copyright © 1994 by TOPS Learning Systems, Canby OR 97013. Reproduction limited to personal classroom use.

GALAXY RULER
ACTIVITY 20

MILKY WAY DISK
ACTIVITY 20

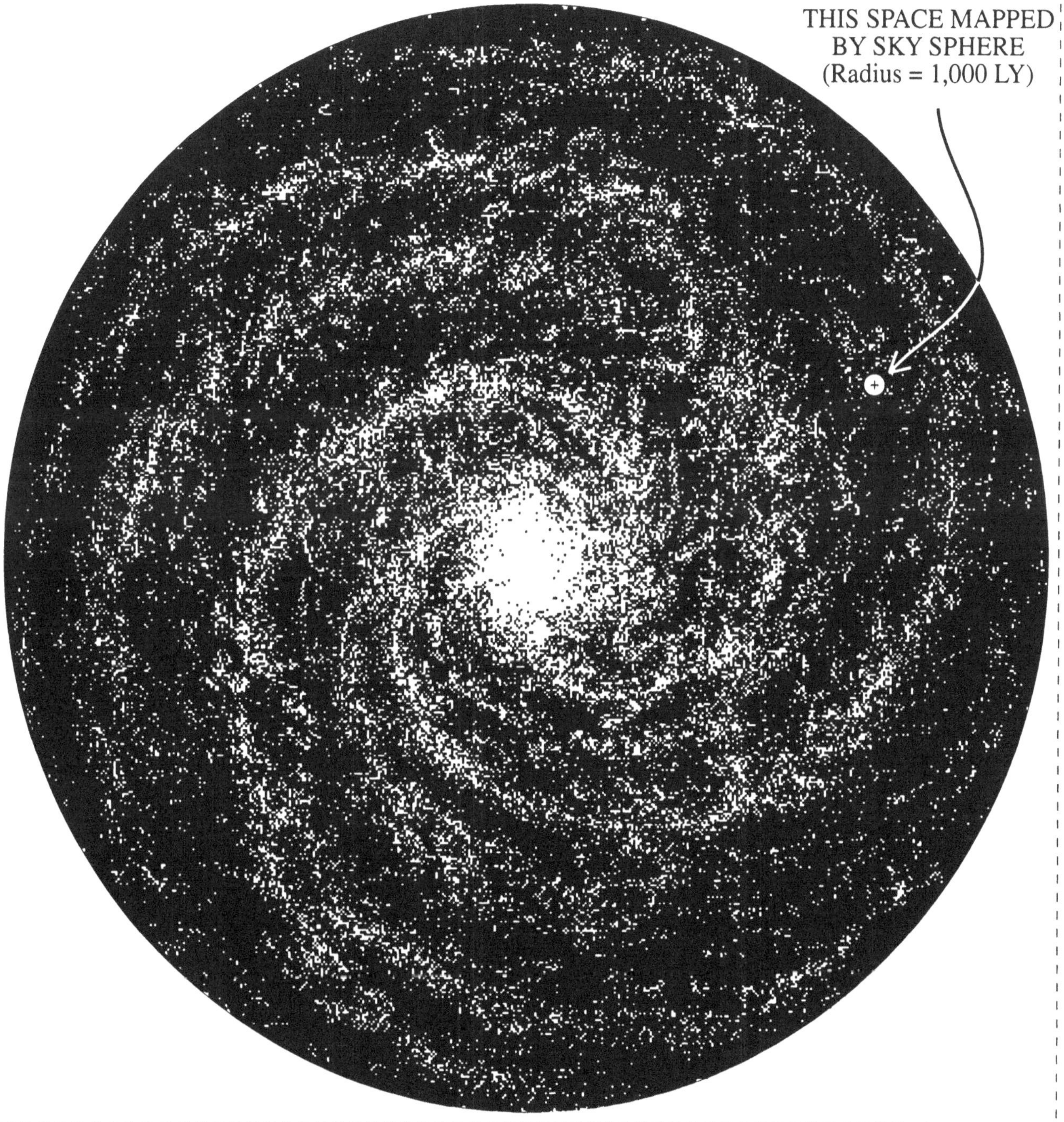

THIS SPACE MAPPED BY SKY SPHERE (Radius = 1,000 LY)

Copyright © 1994 by TOPS Learning Systems, Canby OR 97013. Reproduction limited to personal classroom use.

Feedback

If you enjoyed teaching TOPS please tell us so. Your praise motivates us to work hard. If you found an error or can suggest ways to improve this module, we need to hear about that too. Your criticism will help us improve our next new edition. Would you like information about our other publications? Ask us to send you our latest catalog free of charge.

For whatever reason, we'd love to hear from you. We include this self-mailer for your convenience.

Ron and Peg Marson

author and illustrator

Your Message Here:

Module Title _____ Date _____

Name _____ School _____

Address _____

City _____ State _____ Zip _____

———————————————— FIRST FOLD ————————————————

———————————————— SECOND FOLD ————————————————

RETURN ADDRESS

_____
_____
_____

PLACE
STAMP
HERE

TOPS Learning Systems
342 S Plumas Street
Willows, CA 95988

TAPE HERE

www.ingramcontent.com/pod-product-compliance
Lightning Source LLC
Chambersburg PA
CBHW081827170426
43202CB00019B/2976